TEACHER'S PET PUBLICATIONS

PUZZLE PACK
for
The Grapes of Wrath

based on the book by
John Steinbeck

Written by
William T. Collins

© 2005 Teacher's Pet Publications
All Rights Reserved

The materials in this packet are copyrighted
by Teacher's Pet Publications, Inc.

These pages may be duplicated by the purchaser
for use in the purchaser's own classroom.

Copying any of these materials and distributing them
for any other purpose is a violation of the copyright laws.

© 2005 Teacher's Pet Publications, Inc.
www.tpet.com

INTRODUCTION
If you already own the LitPlan for this title, this Puzzle Pack will refresh your Unit Resource Materials and Vocabulary Resource Materials sections plus give you additional materials you can substitute into the tests. If you do not already have a complete LitPlan, these pages will give you some supplemental materials to use with your own plan. There are two main groups of materials: one set for unit words (such as characters' names, symbols, places, etc.) and one set for vocabulary words associated with the book.

WORD LIST
There is a word list for both the unit words and the vocabulary words. These lists show you which words are being used in the materials and the clues or definitions being used for those words. You may want to give students a word list with clues/definitions to help them, or you may want students to only have a word list (without clues/definitions) if you want them to work a little harder. Both are available for duplication. The word lists can also be your "calling key" for the bingo games.

FILL IN THE BLANK AND MATCHING
There are 4 each of the fill in the blank and matching worksheets for both the unit and vocabulary words. These pages can be used either as extra worksheets for students or as objective parts of a unit test. They can be done individually if students need extra help or as a whole class activity to review the material covered.

MAGIC SQUARES
The magic squares not only reinforce the material covered but also work on reasoning and math skills. Many teachers have told us that their students really enjoy doing these!

WORD SEARCH PUZZLES
The word search words go in all directions, as indicated on your answer keys. Two of the word search puzzles have the clues listed rather than the words. This makes the puzzle a little more difficult, but it reinforces the material better. Two word search puzzles have words only for students who find the clue puzzles too difficult.

CROSSWORD PUZZLES
Both unit and vocabulary word sections have 4 crossword puzzles.

BINGO CARDS
There are 32 individual bingo cards for the unit words and 32 individual bingo cards for the vocabulary words. You can use your word list as a "call list," calling the words at random and marking them off of your list as you go, or you could use the flash cards by cutting them apart and drawing the words at random from a hat (or box or whatever). To make a better review, you might ask for the definition and spelling of each word as you call it out–or you could call out the definitions and have students tell you the words they need to look for on the puzzle.

JUGGLE LETTERS
The vocabulary juggle letter game is intended to help students learn the spellings of the words. One sheet has the definitions listed on it as an extra help for students who need it or to reinforce the definitions if you choose to do so.

FLASH CARDS
We've included a set of vocabulary flash cards you can duplicate, cut, and fold for your students. Some teachers make a few sets for general use by the class; others make a set for each student. Some teachers duplicate them for each student and have the students cut & fold their own. You can cut out just the words and put them in a hat, have each student pick out one word and write the definition and a sentence for that word. Students then swap words and papers, with the next student adding a sentence of his own under the last one. You can have students swap as many times as you like. Each time the student will read the sentences written prior to his own and then add a sentence. You can cut out the words and definitions separately and play "I Have; Who Has?" Each student in the room draws a word and definition. The first student says, "I have (the name of the word). Who has the definition?" The student with the definition reads it then says, "I have (the name of the vocabulary word she has). Who has the definition?" The round continues until all words and definitions have been given.

Copyrighted

Grapes of Wrath Word List

No.	Word	Clue/Definition
1.	BABY	It was born dead
2.	BARN	Last place of shelter where the Joads found an old man
3.	CALIFORNIA	The Joads' destination
4.	CAMP	Place to pitch a tent and spend the night
5.	CASY	Jim's last name
6.	CLUB	Tom used one to smash the head of one of Casy's attackers
7.	CONNIE	He planned to study a trade but left instead
8.	COTTON	The Joads went to pick it after peaches
9.	DAY	Take one ___ at a time and don't worry about the future
10.	DEPRESSION	Era in American history in which the story is set
11.	DEPUTY	Casy kicked him so Tom could get away
12.	DESERT	Hot, dry land Joads crossed to get to California
13.	FAMILY	Ma Joad believed that the ___ should stay together
14.	FLOOD	Too much rain caused one
15.	FRUIT	Tons of it were left to rot
16.	GRANDMA	She died just before the agricultural inspection station
17.	GRAPES	The ___ of Wrath
18.	HOOVERVILLE	Nickname for camp for migrant workers
19.	JIM	Former preacher
20.	JOHN	His wife died from a burst appendix
21.	MA	Mrs. Joad
22.	MIGRANT	Kind of workers who move from place to place
23.	MONEY	The Joads had to find work to get it to buy food
24.	MONSTER	The banking industry was the ___ that men could not control
25.	MOUNTAINS	The Rockies, for example
26.	MULEY	Mr. Graves
27.	NOAH	He had a strange sense of calmness about him
28.	PA	Mr. Joad
29.	PEACHES	The Joads picked them from trees
30.	RAGGED	The ___ man told about low wages & starving families
31.	RIVER	It ran over its banks and flooded the whole area
32.	RUTHIE	She told on Tom
33.	SHARON	She was pregnant; Rose of ___
34.	SIN	There ain't no ___ and there ain't no virtue
35.	STEINBECK	Author
36.	STRIKE	Workers at the peach orchard went on ___ for higher wages
37.	THOMAS	He lowered wages from .30 to .25 per hour
38.	TIRE	While the Joads were stopped to fix it, a man told them about work to the north
39.	TOM	He was recently released on parole
40.	TRACTOR	Big ones are used to help cultivate the land
41.	TURTLE	It was determined to climb the bank to the road
42.	WILSONS	They offered their tent to Grandpa
43.	WINFIELD	He got sick eating peaches
44.	WORK	Everyone was looking for ___; a job
45.	WRATH	The Grapes of ___

The Grapes of Wrath Fill In The Blank 1

_____ 1. Last place of shelter where the Joads found an old man

_____ 2. Tom used one to smash the head of one of Casy's attackers

_____ 3. They offered their tent to Grandpa

_____ 4. Big ones are used to help cultivate the land

_____ 5. It was determined to climb the bank to the road

_____ 6. The ___ man told about low wages & starving families

_____ 7. Casy kicked him so Tom could get away

_____ 8. He got sick eating peaches

_____ 9. She died just before the agricultural inspection station

_____ 10. The Joads went to pick it after peaches

_____ 11. Mr. Graves

_____ 12. He had a strange sense of calmness about him

_____ 13. Mrs. Joad

_____ 14. It was born dead

_____ 15. Author

_____ 16. The Rockies, for example

_____ 17. Take one ___ at a time and don't worry about the future

_____ 18. It ran over its banks and flooded the whole area

_____ 19. The Joads had to find work to get it to buy food

_____ 20. He planned to study a trade but left instead

The Grapes of Wrath Fill In The Blank 1 Answer Key

BARN	1. Last place of shelter where the Joads found an old man
CLUB	2. Tom used one to smash the head of one of Casy's attackers
WILSONS	3. They offered their tent to Grandpa
TRACTOR	4. Big ones are used to help cultivate the land
TURTLE	5. It was determined to climb the bank to the road
RAGGED	6. The ___ man told about low wages & starving families
DEPUTY	7. Casy kicked him so Tom could get away
WINFIELD	8. He got sick eating peaches
GRANDMA	9. She died just before the agricultural inspection station
COTTON	10. The Joads went to pick it after peaches
MULEY	11. Mr. Graves
NOAH	12. He had a strange sense of calmness about him
MA	13. Mrs. Joad
BABY	14. It was born dead
STEINBECK	15. Author
MOUNTAINS	16. The Rockies, for example
DAY	17. Take one ___ at a time and don't worry about the future
RIVER	18. It ran over its banks and flooded the whole area
MONEY	19. The Joads had to find work to get it to buy food
CONNIE	20. He planned to study a trade but left instead

The Grapes of Wrath Fill in The Blank 2

_____ 1. The Rockies, for example

_____ 2. Jim's last name

_____ 3. Tom used one to smash the head of one of Casy's attackers

_____ 4. He was recently released on parole

_____ 5. Tons of it were left to rot

_____ 6. Big ones are used to help cultivate the land

_____ 7. It ran over its banks and flooded the whole area

_____ 8. His wife died from a burst appendix

_____ 9. He lowered wages from .30 to .25 per hour

_____ 10. The ___ of Wrath

_____ 11. Former preacher

_____ 12. Too much rain caused one

_____ 13. Take one ___ at a time and don't worry about the future

_____ 14. Mr. Joad

_____ 15. The Joads' destination

_____ 16. She was pregnant; Rose of ___

_____ 17. He planned to study a trade but left instead

_____ 18. It was born dead

_____ 19. Casy kicked him so Tom could get away

_____ 20. She died just before the agricultural inspection station

The Grapes of Wrath Fill In The Blank 2 Answer Key

MOUNTAINS	1. The Rockies, for example
CASY	2. Jim's last name
CLUB	3. Tom used one to smash the head of one of Casy's attackers
TOM	4. He was recently released on parole
FRUIT	5. Tons of it were left to rot
TRACTOR	6. Big ones are used to help cultivate the land
RIVER	7. It ran over its banks and flooded the whole area
JOHN	8. His wife died from a burst appendix
THOMAS	9. He lowered wages from .30 to .25 per hour
GRAPES	10. The ___ of Wrath
JIM	11. Former preacher
FLOOD	12. Too much rain caused one
DAY	13. Take one ___ at a time and don't worry about the future
PA	14. Mr. Joad
CALIFORNIA	15. The Joads' destination
SHARON	16. She was pregnant; Rose of ___
CONNIE	17. He planned to study a trade but left instead
BABY	18. It was born dead
DEPUTY	19. Casy kicked him so Tom could get away
GRANDMA	20. She died just before the agricultural inspection station

The Grapes of Wrath Fill In The Blank 3

1. While the Joads were stopped to fix it, a man told them about work to the north
2. He planned to study a trade but left instead
3. It ran over its banks and flooded the whole area
4. Tom used one to smash the head of one of Casy's attackers
5. Jim's last name
6. She died just before the agricultural inspection station
7. It was born dead
8. Everyone was looking for ___; a job
9. Mr. Graves
10. His wife died from a burst appendix
11. Kind of workers who move from place to place
12. The Joads' destination
13. Former preacher
14. There ain't no ___ and there ain't no virtue
15. Place to pitch a tent and spend the night
16. He was recently released on parole
17. Ma Joad believed that the ___ should stay together
18. The ___ man told about low wages & starving families
19. Last place of shelter where the Joads found an old man
20. Nickname for camp for migrant workers

The Grapes of Wrath Fill In The Blank 3 Answer Key

TIRE	1. While the Joads were stopped to fix it, a man told them about work to the north
CONNIE	2. He planned to study a trade but left instead
RIVER	3. It ran over its banks and flooded the whole area
CLUB	4. Tom used one to smash the head of one of Casy's attackers
CASY	5. Jim's last name
GRANDMA	6. She died just before the agricultural inspection station
BABY	7. It was born dead
WORK	8. Everyone was looking for ___; a job
MULEY	9. Mr. Graves
JOHN	10. His wife died from a burst appendix
MIGRANT	11. Kind of workers who move from place to place
CALIFORNIA	12. The Joads' destination
JIM	13. Former preacher
SIN	14. There ain't no ___ and there ain't no virtue
CAMP	15. Place to pitch a tent and spend the night
TOM	16. He was recently released on parole
FAMILY	17. Ma Joad believed that the ___ should stay together
RAGGED	18. The ___ man told about low wages & starving families
BARN	19. Last place of shelter where the Joads found an old man
HOOVERVILLE	20. Nickname for camp for migrant workers

The Grapes of Wrath Fill In The Blank 4

1. There ain't no ___ and there ain't no virtue
2. The ___ of Wrath
3. Mr. Joad
4. Nickname for camp for migrant workers
5. Mr. Graves
6. She told on Tom
7. Hot, dry land Joads crossed to get to California
8. It was born dead
9. His wife died from a burst appendix
10. The Joads' destination
11. The Rockies, for example
12. Take one ___ at a time and don't worry about the future
13. Last place of shelter where the Joads found an old man
14. Casy kicked him so Tom could get away
15. Mrs. Joad
16. He had a strange sense of calmness about him
17. Workers at the peach orchard went on ___ for higher wages
18. Tons of it were left to rot
19. Author
20. Jim's last name

The Grapes of Wrath Fill In The Blank 4 Answer key

SIN	1. There ain't no ___ and there ain't no virtue
GRAPES	2. The ___ of Wrath
PA	3. Mr. Joad
HOOVERVILLE	4. Nickname for camp for migrant workers
MULEY	5. Mr. Graves
RUTHIE	6. She told on Tom
DESERT	7. Hot, dry land Joads crossed to get to California
BABY	8. It was born dead
JOHN	9. His wife died from a burst appendix
CALIFORNIA	10. The Joads' destination
MOUNTAINS	11. The Rockies, for example
DAY	12. Take one ___ at a time and don't worry about the future
BARN	13. Last place of shelter where the Joads found an old man
DEPUTY	14. Casy kicked him so Tom could get away
MA	15. Mrs. Joad
NOAH	16. He had a strange sense of calmness about him
STRIKE	17. Workers at the peach orchard went on ___ for higher wages
FRUIT	18. Tons of it were left to rot
STEINBECK	19. Author
CASY	20. Jim's last name

Copyrighted

The Grapes of Wrath Matching 1

___ 1. MA   A. Jim's last name
___ 2. WRATH   B. It was born dead
___ 3. MULEY   C. Workers at the peach orchard went on ___ for higher wages
___ 4. GRAPES   D. Take one ___ at a time and don't worry about the future
___ 5. RUTHIE   E. It was determined to climb the bank to the road
___ 6. TRACTOR   F. Tons of it were left to rot
___ 7. TURTLE   G. Mrs. Joad
___ 8. RIVER   H. The Joads picked them from trees
___ 9. DESERT   I. She told on Tom
___ 10. DAY   J. They offered their tent to Grandpa
___ 11. FRUIT   K. Casy kicked him so Tom could get away
___ 12. PEACHES   L. The Grapes of ___
___ 13. JOHN   M. Last place of shelter where the Joads found an old man
___ 14. BABY   N. His wife died from a burst appendix
___ 15. TOM   O. Mr. Joad
___ 16. DEPUTY   P. He was recently released on parole
___ 17. BARN   Q. Hot, dry land Joads crossed to get to California
___ 18. WILSONS   R. The ___ of Wrath
___ 19. PA   S. The Joads had to find work to get it to buy food
___ 20. STRIKE   T. Big ones are used to help cultivate the land
___ 21. CALIFORNIA   U. He lowered wages from .30 to .25 per hour
___ 22. MONEY   V. She died just before the agricultural inspection station
___ 23. CASY   W. It ran over its banks and flooded the whole area
___ 24. GRANDMA   X. Mr. Graves
___ 25. THOMAS   Y. The Joads' destination

The Grapes of Wrath Matching 1 Answer Key

G - 1.	MA	A. Jim's last name
L - 2.	WRATH	B. It was born dead
X - 3.	MULEY	C. Workers at the peach orchard went on ___ for higher wages
R - 4.	GRAPES	D. Take one ___ at a time and don't worry about the future
I - 5.	RUTHIE	E. It was determined to climb the bank to the road
T - 6.	TRACTOR	F. Tons of it were left to rot
E - 7.	TURTLE	G. Mrs. Joad
W - 8.	RIVER	H. The Joads picked them from trees
Q - 9.	DESERT	I. She told on Tom
D - 10.	DAY	J. They offered their tent to Grandpa
F - 11.	FRUIT	K. Casy kicked him so Tom could get away
H - 12.	PEACHES	L. The Grapes of ___
N - 13.	JOHN	M. Last place of shelter where the Joads found an old man
B - 14.	BABY	N. His wife died from a burst appendix
P - 15.	TOM	O. Mr. Joad
K - 16.	DEPUTY	P. He was recently released on parole
M - 17.	BARN	Q. Hot, dry land Joads crossed to get to California
J - 18.	WILSONS	R. The ___ of Wrath
O - 19.	PA	S. The Joads had to find work to get it to buy food
C - 20.	STRIKE	T. Big ones are used to help cultivate the land
Y - 21.	CALIFORNIA	U. He lowered wages from .30 to .25 per hour
S - 22.	MONEY	V. She died just before the agricultural inspection station
A - 23.	CASY	W. It ran over its banks and flooded the whole area
V - 24.	GRANDMA	X. Mr. Graves
U - 25.	THOMAS	Y. The Joads' destination

The Grapes of Wrath Matching 2

___ 1. HOOVERVILLE A. The banking industry was the ___ that men could not control
___ 2. MONEY B. The Joads picked them from trees
___ 3. TOM C. The Grapes of ___
___ 4. CONNIE D. He planned to study a trade but left instead
___ 5. NOAH E. Jim's last name
___ 6. WRATH F. Nickname for camp for migrant workers
___ 7. GRANDMA G. Author
___ 8. GRAPES H. They offered their tent to Grandpa
___ 9. STEINBECK I. Tom used one to smash the head of one of Casy's attackers
___10. DAY J. The Joads had to find work to get it to buy food
___11. CASY K. The ___ of Wrath
___12. STRIKE L. Place to pitch a tent and spend the night
___13. BABY M. Workers at the peach orchard went on ___ for higher wages
___14. WILSONS N. Take one ___ at a time and don't worry about the future
___15. MONSTER O. Former preacher
___16. CAMP P. He was recently released on parole
___17. TIRE Q. The Joads' destination
___18. CLUB R. She died just before the agricultural inspection station
___19. SIN S. Hot, dry land Joads crossed to get to California
___20. DESERT T. He lowered wages from .30 to .25 per hour
___21. JIM U. Mr. Graves
___22. CALIFORNIA V. While the Joads were stopped to fix it, a man told them about work to the north
___23. THOMAS W. There ain't no ___ and there ain't no virtue
___24. PEACHES X. He had a strange sense of calmness about him
___25. MULEY Y. It was born dead

The Grapes of Wrath Matching 2 Answer Key

F - 1.	HOOVERVILLE	A. The banking industry was the ___ that men could not control
J - 2.	MONEY	B. The Joads picked them from trees
P - 3.	TOM	C. The Grapes of ____
D - 4.	CONNIE	D. He planned to study a trade but left instead
X - 5.	NOAH	E. Jim's last name
C - 6.	WRATH	F. Nickname for camp for migrant workers
R - 7.	GRANDMA	G. Author
K - 8.	GRAPES	H. They offered their tent to Grandpa
G - 9.	STEINBECK	I. Tom used one to smash the head of one of Casy's attackers
N - 10.	DAY	J. The Joads had to find work to get it to buy food
E - 11.	CASY	K. The ___ of Wrath
M - 12.	STRIKE	L. Place to pitch a tent and spend the night
Y - 13.	BABY	M. Workers at the peach orchard went on ___ for higher wages
H - 14.	WILSONS	N. Take one ___ at a time and don't worry about the future
A - 15.	MONSTER	O. Former preacher
L - 16.	CAMP	P. He was recently released on parole
V - 17.	TIRE	Q. The Joads' destination
I - 18.	CLUB	R. She died just before the agricultural inspection station
W - 19.	SIN	S. Hot, dry land Joads crossed to get to California
S - 20.	DESERT	T. He lowered wages from .30 to .25 per hour
O - 21.	JIM	U. Mr. Graves
Q - 22.	CALIFORNIA	V. While the Joads were stopped to fix it, a man told them about work to the north
T - 23.	THOMAS	W. There ain't no ___ and there ain't no virtue
B - 24.	PEACHES	X. He had a strange sense of calmness about him
U - 25.	MULEY	Y. It was born dead

Copyrighted

The Grapes of Wrath Matching 3

___ 1. WORK   A. Casy kicked him so Tom could get away
___ 2. TIRE   B. The ___ of Wrath
___ 3. JOHN   C. The Joads went to pick it after peaches
___ 4. CAS   D. Nickname for camp for migrant workers
___ 5. FLOOD   E. The Rockies, for example
___ 6. MIGRANT   F. It was born dead
___ 7. RAGGED   G. He lowered wages from .30 to .25 per hour
___ 8. TURTLE   H. Mr. Joad
___ 9. MOUNTAINS   I. Former preacher
___10. DESERT   J. Kind of workers who move from place to place
___11. RIVER   K. They offered their tent to Grandpa
___12. JIM   L. It ran over its banks and flooded the whole area
___13. BABY   M. Hot, dry land Joads crossed to get to California
___14. COTTON   N. Tons of it were left to rot
___15. GRAPES   O. He had a strange sense of calmness about him
___16. DEPUTY   P. Too much rain caused one
___17. PA   Q. She told on Tom
___18. RUTHIE   R. The ___ man told about low wages & starving families
___19. THOMAS   S. The Joads' destination
___20. CALIFORNIA   T. Everyone was looking for ___; a job
___21. WILSONS   U. While the Joads were stopped to fix it, a man told them about work to the north
___22. NOAH   V. His wife died from a burst appendix
___23. FRUIT   W. The Grapes of ___
___24. WRATH   X. It was determined to climb the bank to the road
___25. HOOVERVILLE   Y. Jim's last name

The Grapes of Wrath Matching 3 Answer Key

T - 1.	WORK	A. Casy kicked him so Tom could get away
U - 2.	TIRE	B. The ___ of Wrath
V - 3.	JOHN	C. The Joads went to pick it after peaches
Y - 4.	CASY	D. Nickname for camp for migrant workers
P - 5.	FLOOD	E. The Rockies, for example
J - 6.	MIGRANT	F. It was born dead
R - 7.	RAGGED	G. He lowered wages from .30 to .25 per hour
X - 8.	TURTLE	H. Mr. Joad
E - 9.	MOUNTAINS	I. Former preacher
M - 10.	DESERT	J. Kind of workers who move from place to place
L - 11.	RIVER	K. They offered their tent to Grandpa
I - 12.	JIM	L. It ran over its banks and flooded the whole area
F - 13.	BABY	M. Hot, dry land Joads crossed to get to California
C - 14.	COTTON	N. Tons of it were left to rot
B - 15.	GRAPES	O. He had a strange sense of calmness about him
A - 16.	DEPUTY	P. Too much rain caused one
H - 17.	PA	Q. She told on Tom
Q - 18.	RUTHIE	R. The ___ man told about low wages & starving families
G - 19.	THOMAS	S. The Joads' destination
S - 20.	CALIFORNIA	T. Everyone was looking for ___; a job
K - 21.	WILSONS	U. While the Joads were stopped to fix it, a man told them about work to the north
O - 22.	NOAH	V. His wife died from a burst appendix
N - 23.	FRUIT	W. The Grapes of ___
W - 24.	WRATH	X. It was determined to climb the bank to the road
D - 25.	HOOVERVILLE	Y. Jim's last name

The Grapes of Wrath Matching 4

___ 1. HOOVERVILLE
___ 2. DESERT
___ 3. MONSTER
___ 4. GRANDMA
___ 5. TIRE
___ 6. MA
___ 7. TOM
___ 8. DEPRESSION
___ 9. TRACTOR
___ 10. TURTLE
___ 11. COTTON
___ 12. FAMILY
___ 13. GRAPES
___ 14. CASY
___ 15. RIVER
___ 16. THOMAS
___ 17. JIM
___ 18. WRATH
___ 19. JOHN
___ 20. SIN
___ 21. CLUB
___ 22. MONEY
___ 23. FRUIT
___ 24. NOAH
___ 25. WINFIELD

A. He had a strange sense of calmness about him
B. Tons of it were left to rot
C. The Joads went to pick it after peaches
D. The banking industry was the ___ that men could not control
E. The Joads had to find work to get it to buy food
F. He lowered wages from .30 to .25 per hour
G. The ___ of Wrath
H. Ma Joad believed that the ___ should stay together
I. The Grapes of ___
J. He got sick eating peaches
K. Jim's last name
L. Era in American history in which the story is set
M. Former preacher
N. Tom used one to smash the head of one of Casy's attackers
O. While the Joads were stopped to fix it, a man told them about work to the north
P. His wife died from a burst appendix
Q. There ain't no ___ and there ain't no virtue
R. Big ones are used to help cultivate the land
S. She died just before the agricultural inspection station
T. Nickname for camp for migrant workers
U. He was recently released on parole
V. It was determined to climb the bank to the road
W. It ran over its banks and flooded the whole area
X. Mrs. Joad
Y. Hot, dry land Joads crossed to get to California

The Grapes of Wrath Matching 4 Answer Key

T - 1. HOOVERVILLE	A. He had a strange sense of calmness about him
Y - 2. DESERT	B. Tons of it were left to rot
D - 3. MONSTER	C. The Joads went to pick it after peaches
S - 4. GRANDMA	D. The banking industry was the ___ that men could not control
O - 5. TIRE	E. The Joads had to find work to get it to buy food
X - 6. MA	F. He lowered wages from .30 to .25 per hour
U - 7. TOM	G. The ___ of Wrath
L - 8. DEPRESSION	H. Ma Joad believed that the ___ should stay together
R - 9. TRACTOR	I. The Grapes of ___
V - 10. TURTLE	J. He got sick eating peaches
C - 11. COTTON	K. Jim's last name
H - 12. FAMILY	L. Era in American history in which the story is set
G - 13. GRAPES	M. Former preacher
K - 14. CASY	N. Tom used one to smash the head of one of Casy's attackers
W - 15. RIVER	O. While the Joads were stopped to fix it, a man told them about work to the north
F - 16. THOMAS	P. His wife died from a burst appendix
M - 17. JIM	Q. There ain't no ___ and there ain't no virtue
I - 18. WRATH	R. Big ones are used to help cultivate the land
P - 19. JOHN	S. She died just before the agricultural inspection station
Q - 20. SIN	T. Nickname for camp for migrant workers
N - 21. CLUB	U. He was recently released on parole
E - 22. MONEY	V. It was determined to climb the bank to the road
B - 23. FRUIT	W. It ran over its banks and flooded the whole area
A - 24. NOAH	X. Mrs. Joad
J - 25. WINFIELD	Y. Hot, dry land Joads crossed to get to California

The Grapes of Wrath Magic Squares 1

Match the definition with the vocabulary word. Put your answers in the magic squares below. When your answers are correct, all columns and rows will add to the same number.

A. PEACHES E. MA   I. CONNIE   M. BARN
B. GRAPES   F. CASY   J. DAY   N. TOM
C. WRATH   G. DEPRESSION K. RIVER   O. DEPUTY
D. TIRE   H. PA   L. MIGRANT   P. TRACTOR

1. Mr. Joad
2. The Joads picked them from trees
3. The ___ of Wrath
4. Era in American history in which the story is set
5. Take one ___ at a time and don't worry about the future
6. Casy kicked him so Tom could get away
7. Big ones are used to help cultivate the land
8. He planned to study a trade but left instead
9. It ran over its banks and flooded the whole area
10. He was recently released on parole
11. Last place of shelter where the Joads found an old man
12. Kind of workers who move from place to place
13. Mrs. Joad
14. While the Joads were stopped to fix it, a man told them about work to the north
15. The Grapes of ____
16. Jim's last name

A=	B=	C=	D=
E=	F=	G=	H=
I=	J=	K=	L=
M=	N=	O=	P=

The Grapes of Wrath Magic Squares 1 Answer Key

Match the definition with the vocabulary word. Put your answers in the magic squares below. When your answers are correct, all columns and rows will add to the same number.

A. PEACHES
B. GRAPES
C. WRATH
D. TIRE
E. MA
F. CASY
G. DEPRESSION
H. PA
I. CONNIE
J. DAY
K. RIVER
L. MIGRANT
M. BARN
N. TOM
O. DEPUTY
P. TRACTOR

1. Mr. Joad
2. The Joads picked them from trees
3. The ___ of Wrath
4. Era in American history in which the story is set
5. Take one ___ at a time and don't worry about the future
6. Casy kicked him so Tom could get away
7. Big ones are used to help cultivate the land
8. He planned to study a trade but left instead
9. It ran over its banks and flooded the whole area
10. He was recently released on parole
11. Last place of shelter where the Joads found an old man
12. Kind of workers who move from place to place
13. Mrs. Joad
14. While the Joads were stopped to fix it, a man told them about work to the north
15. The Grapes of ___
16. Jim's last name

A=2	B=3	C=15	D=14
E=13	F=16	G=4	H=1
I=8	J=5	K=9	L=12
M=11	N=10	O=6	P=7

The Grapes of Wrath Magic Squares 2

Match the definition with the vocabulary word. Put your answers in the magic squares below. When your answers are correct, all columns and rows will add to the same number.

A. STEINBECK E. CLUB   I. WRATH   M. FAMILY
B. COTTON   F. CASY   J. WORK   N. RUTHIE
C. MOUNTAINS G. JOHN   K. FRUIT   O. DEPRESSION
D. PA   H. GRANDMA L. SHARON P. HOOVERVILLE

1. The Rockies, for example
2. Everyone was looking for ___; a job
3. Jim's last name
4. Era in American history in which the story is set
5. Nickname for camp for migrant workers
6. Tom used one to smash the head of one of Casy's attackers
7. The Grapes of ____
8. Mr. Joad
9. Ma Joad believed that the ___ should stay together
10. She died just before the agricultural inspection station
11. She was pregnant; Rose of ___
12. Author
13. The Joads went to pick it after peaches
14. Tons of it were left to rot
15. His wife died from a burst appendix
16. She told on Tom

A=	B=	C=	D=
E=	F=	G=	H=
I=	J=	K=	L=
M=	N=	O=	P=

The Grapes of Wrath Magic Squares 2 Answer Key

Match the definition with the vocabulary word. Put your answers in the magic squares below. When your answers are correct, all columns and rows will add to the same number.

A. STEINBECK
B. COTTON
C. MOUNTAINS
D. PA
E. CLUB
F. CASY
G. JOHN
H. GRANDMA
I. WRATH
J. WORK
K. FRUIT
L. SHARON
M. FAMILY
N. RUTHIE
O. DEPRESSION
P. HOOVERVILLE

1. The Rockies, for example
2. Everyone was looking for ___; a job
3. Jim's last name
4. Era in American history in which the story is set
5. Nickname for camp for migrant workers
6. Tom used one to smash the head of one of Casy's attackers
7. The Grapes of ____
8. Mr. Joad
9. Ma Joad believed that the ___ should stay together
10. She died just before the agricultural inspection station
11. She was pregnant; Rose of ___
12. Author
13. The Joads went to pick it after peaches
14. Tons of it were left to rot
15. His wife died from a burst appendix
16. She told on Tom

A=12	B=13	C=1	D=8
E=6	F=3	G=15	H=10
I=7	J=2	K=14	L=11
M=9	N=16	O=4	P=5

The Grapes of Wrath Magic Squares 3

Match the definition with the vocabulary word. Put your answers in the magic squares below. When your answers are correct, all columns and rows will add to the same number.

A. WINFIELD
B. STEINBECK
C. GRANDMA
D. MIGRANT
E. JIM
F. MOUNTAINS
G. MONSTER
H. COTTON
I. BARN
J. CLUB
K. TURTLE
L. WRATH
M. FLOOD
N. FRUIT
O. RAGGED
P. JOHN

1. The ___ man told about low wages & starving families
2. Tom used one to smash the head of one of Casy's attackers
3. The Joads went to pick it after peaches
4. He got sick eating peaches
5. Kind of workers who move from place to place
6. Former preacher
7. It was determined to climb the bank to the road
8. Tons of it were left to rot
9. The Rockies, for example
10. She died just before the agricultural inspection station
11. Too much rain caused one
12. The Grapes of ____
13. Last place of shelter where the Joads found an old man
14. His wife died from a burst appendix
15. Author
16. The banking industry was the ___ that men could not control

A=	B=	C=	D=
E=	F=	G=	H=
I=	J=	K=	L=
M=	N=	O=	P=

The Grapes of Wrath Magic Squares 3 Answer Key

Match the definition with the vocabulary word. Put your answers in the magic squares below. When your answers are correct, all columns and rows will add to the same number.

A. WINFIELD
B. STEINBECK
C. GRANDMA
D. MIGRANT
E. JIM
F. MOUNTAINS
G. MONSTER
H. COTTON
I. BARN
J. CLUB
K. TURTLE
L. WRATH
M. FLOOD
N. FRUIT
O. RAGGED
P. JOHN

1. The ___ man told about low wages & starving families
2. Tom used one to smash the head of one of Casy's attackers
3. The Joads went to pick it after peaches
4. He got sick eating peaches
5. Kind of workers who move from place to place
6. Former preacher
7. It was determined to climb the bank to the road
8. Tons of it were left to rot
9. The Rockies, for example
10. She died just before the agricultural inspection station
11. Too much rain caused one
12. The Grapes of ___
13. Last place of shelter where the Joads found an old man
14. His wife died from a burst appendix
15. Author
16. The banking industry was the ___ that men could not control

A=4	B=15	C=10	D=5
E=6	F=9	G=16	H=3
I=13	J=2	K=7	L=12
M=11	N=8	O=1	P=14

The Grapes of Wrath Magic Squares 4

Match the definition with the vocabulary word. Put your answers in the magic squares below. When your answers are correct, all columns and rows will add to the same number.

A. WRATH   E. FLOOD   I. RIVER   M. BARN
B. CASY   F. DAY   J. WILSONS   N. SIN
C. WINFIELD   G. DEPUTY   K. DEPRESSION   O. MOUNTAINS
D. JOHN   H. MULEY   L. THOMAS   P. MONEY

1. The Grapes of ____
2. There ain't no ___ and there ain't no virtue
3. They offered their tent to Grandpa
4. Too much rain caused one
5. Casy kicked him so Tom could get away
6. He lowered wages from .30 to .25 per hour
7. The Joads had to find work to get it to buy food
8. He got sick eating peaches
9. The Rockies, for example
10. His wife died from a burst appendix
11. Mr. Graves
12. Era in American history in which the story is set
13. It ran over its banks and flooded the whole area
14. Take one ___ at a time and don't worry about the future
15. Jim's last name
16. Last place of shelter where the Joads found an old man

A=	B=	C=	D=
E=	F=	G=	H=
I=	J=	K=	L=
M=	N=	O=	P=

27
Copyrighted

The Grapes of Wrath Magic Squares 4 Answer Key

Match the definition with the vocabulary word. Put your answers in the magic squares below. When your answers are correct, all columns and rows will add to the same number.

A. WRATH   E. FLOOD   I. RIVER   M. BARN
B. CASY   F. DAY   J. WILSONS   N. SIN
C. WINFIELD   G. DEPUTY   K. DEPRESSION   O. MOUNTAINS
D. JOHN   H. MULEY   L. THOMAS   P. MONEY

1. The Grapes of ____
2. There ain't no ___ and there ain't no virtue
3. They offered their tent to Grandpa
4. Too much rain caused one
5. Casy kicked him so Tom could get away
6. He lowered wages from .30 to .25 per hour
7. The Joads had to find work to get it to buy food
8. He got sick eating peaches
9. The Rockies, for example
10. His wife died from a burst appendix
11. Mr. Graves
12. Era in American history in which the story is set
13. It ran over its banks and flooded the whole area
14. Take one ___ at a time and don't worry about the future
15. Jim's last name
16. Last place of shelter where the Joads found an old man

A=1	B=15	C=8	D=10
E=4	F=14	G=5	H=11
I=13	J=3	K=12	L=6
M=16	N=2	O=9	P=7

Copyrighted

The Grapes of Wrath Word Search 1

```
P E A C H E S D H T A R W S B J H
M M A O J B A T E R R K Q I A N O
H S O N Y Y M X R S B A W N B Z O
Y T W N Z D O S D I E Y C R Y Q V
W B S I S S H H E R K R U T H I E
I Z H E L T T M P C H E T I O L R
N T A J R S E W U F O B P U T R V
F X R B I Q O R T L L T M R I T I
I V O B V M R N Y D E O T F R U L
E C N M E P A W S V G Y O O E R L
L Y L C R R G R A P E S K D N T E
D L B U G G H F H C T W E M Q L D
X I H I B K S M V R A G P O D E T
B M M M N R M J P M G M P N Y T W
C A L I F O R N I A N K P E D W P
L F R R T W A P R G H D X Y W T M
K Z F N H O J H S T E I N B E C K
```

Author (9)
Big ones are used to help cultivate the land (7)
Casy kicked him so Tom could get away (6)
Everyone was looking for ___; a job (4)
Former preacher (3)
He got sick eating peaches (8)
He had a strange sense of calmness about him (4)
He lowered wages from .30 to .25 per hour (6)
He planned to study a trade but left instead (6)
He was recently released on parole (3)
His wife died from a burst appendix (4)
Hot, dry land Joads crossed to get to California (6)
It ran over its banks and flooded the whole area (5)
It was born dead (4)
It was determined to climb the bank to the road (6)
Jim's last name (4)
Kind of workers who move from place to place (7)
Last place of shelter where the Joads found an old man (4)
Ma Joad believed that the ___ should stay together (6)
Mr. Graves (5)
Mr. Joad (2)

Mrs. Joad (2)
Nickname for camp for migrant workers (11)
Place to pitch a tent and spend the night (4)
She told on Tom (6)
She was pregnant; Rose of ___ (6)
Take one ___ at a time and don't worry about the future (3)
The Grapes of ____ (5)
The Joads had to find work to get it to buy food (5)
The Joads picked them from trees (7)
The Joads went to pick it after peaches (6)
The Joads' destination (10)
The ___ man told about low wages & starving families (6)
The ___ of Wrath (6)
The banking industry was the ___ that men could not control (7)
There ain't no ___ and there ain't no virtue (3)
They offered their tent to Grandpa (7)
Tom used one to smash the head of one of Casy's attackers (4)
Tons of it were left to rot (5)
Too much rain caused one (5)
While the Joads were stopped to fix it, a man told them about work to the north (4)
Workers at the peach orchard went on ___ for higher wages (6)

The Grapes of Wrath Word Search 1 Answer Key

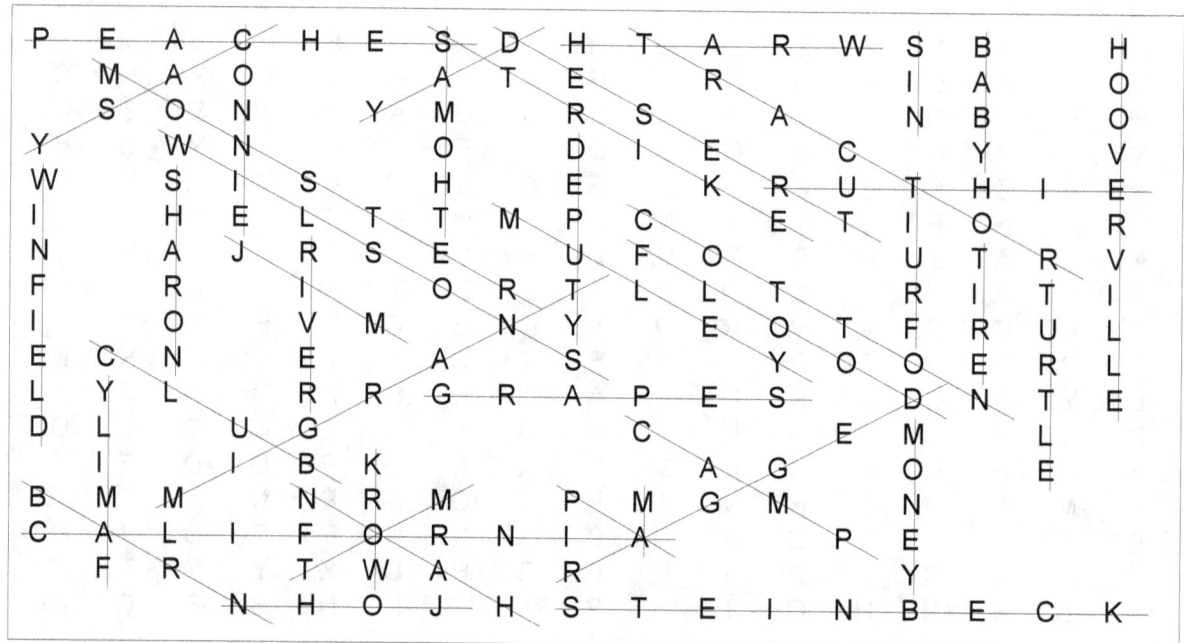

Author (9)
Big ones are used to help cultivate the land (7)
Casy kicked him so Tom could get away (6)
Everyone was looking for ___; a job (4)
Former preacher (3)
He got sick eating peaches (8)
He had a strange sense of calmness about him (4)
He lowered wages from .30 to .25 per hour (6)
He planned to study a trade but left instead (6)
He was recently released on parole (3)
His wife died from a burst appendix (4)
Hot, dry land Joads crossed to get to California (6)
It ran over its banks and flooded the whole area (5)
It was born dead (4)
It was determined to climb the bank to the road (6)
Jim's last name (4)
Kind of workers who move from place to place (7)
Last place of shelter where the Joads found an old man (4)
Ma Joad believed that the ___ should stay together (6)
Mr. Graves (5)
Mr. Joad (2)

Mrs. Joad (2)
Nickname for camp for migrant workers (11)
Place to pitch a tent and spend the night (4)
She told on Tom (6)
She was pregnant; Rose of ___ (6)
Take one ___ at a time and don't worry about the future (3)
The Grapes of ____ (5)
The Joads had to find work to get it to buy food (5)
The Joads picked them from trees (7)
The Joads went to pick it after peaches (6)
The Joads' destination (10)
The ___ man told about low wages & starving families (6)
The ___ of Wrath (6)
The banking industry was the ___ that men could not control (7)
There ain't no ___ and there ain't no virtue (3)
They offered their tent to Grandpa (7)
Tom used one to smash the head of one of Casy's attackers (4)
Tons of it were left to rot (5)
Too much rain caused one (5)
While the Joads were stopped to fix it, a man told them about work to the north (4)
Workers at the peach orchard went on ___ for higher wages (6)

The Grapes of Wrath Word Search 2

```
T U R T L E F N N M T O M J I M D
Z J X I F S O N O O L P A V R O E
C J J Y V R T U T N A Y S S O F P
B D S F A E N D T S Y H W L C F U
S A P H Q T R K O T G E F B R H T
C D S T A H T S C E V R Q U T L Y
W A M I R O J T J R Q I I A D T G
I Y N M U M D E S E R T R W O R K
L S L C T A M I R J R W N K A A H
S M Y W H S O N A B O Z P P M C N
O J I K I S N B G A M H E D V T G
N Z L G E Q E E G R G S N I S O Q
S N B S R D Y C E N G A T V X R P
W L V C P A Z K D C R B N R Q Z R
P P A C O N N I E G U F A M I L Y
R M U L E Y T T W L W T Y B F K C
P R G D Q P E A C H E S X G Y P E
```

Author (9)
Big ones are used to help cultivate the land (7)
Casy kicked him so Tom could get away (6)
Everyone was looking for ___; a job (4)
Former preacher (3)
He had a strange sense of calmness about him (4)
He lowered wages from .30 to .25 per hour (6)
He planned to study a trade but left instead (6)
He was recently released on parole (3)
His wife died from a burst appendix (4)
Hot, dry land Joads crossed to get to California (6)
It ran over its banks and flooded the whole area (5)
It was born dead (4)
It was determined to climb the bank to the road (6)
Jim's last name (4)
Kind of workers who move from place to place (7)
Last place of shelter where the Joads found an old man (4)
Ma Joad believed that the ___ should stay together (6)
Mr. Graves (5)
Mr. Joad (2)
Mrs. Joad (2)

Place to pitch a tent and spend the night (4)
She died just before the agricultural inspection station (7)
She told on Tom (6)
She was pregnant; Rose of ___ (6)
Take one ___ at a time and don't worry about the future (3)
The Grapes of ____ (5)
The Joads had to find work to get it to buy food (5)
The Joads picked them from trees (7)
The Joads went to pick it after peaches (6)
The Rockies, for example (9)
The ___ man told about low wages & starving families (6)
The ___ of Wrath (6)
The banking industry was the ___ that men could not control (7)
There ain't no ___ and there ain't no virtue (3)
They offered their tent to Grandpa (7)
Tom used one to smash the head of one of Casy's attackers (4)
Tons of it were left to rot (5)
Too much rain caused one (5)
While the Joads were stopped to fix it, a man told them about work to the north (4)
Workers at the peach orchard went on ___ for higher wages (6)

The Grapes of Wrath Word Search 2 Answer Key

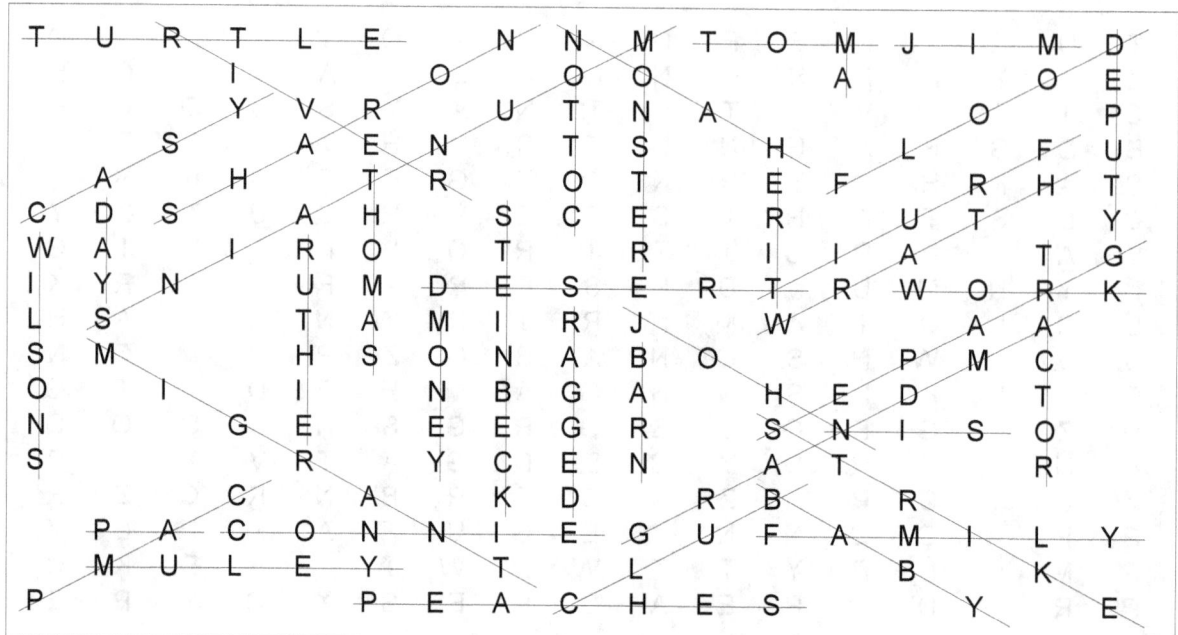

Author (9)
Big ones are used to help cultivate the land (7)
Casy kicked him so Tom could get away (6)
Everyone was looking for ___; a job (4)
Former preacher (3)
He had a strange sense of calmness about him (4)
He lowered wages from .30 to .25 per hour (6)
He planned to study a trade but left instead (6)
He was recently released on parole (3)
His wife died from a burst appendix (4)
Hot, dry land Joads crossed to get to California (6)
It ran over its banks and flooded the whole area (5)
It was born dead (4)
It was determined to climb the bank to the road (6)
Jim's last name (4)
Kind of workers who move from place to place (7)
Last place of shelter where the Joads found an old man (4)
Ma Joad believed that the ___ should stay together (6)
Mr. Graves (5)
Mr. Joad (2)
Mrs. Joad (2)

Place to pitch a tent and spend the night (4)
She died just before the agricultural inspection station (7)
She told on Tom (6)
She was pregnant; Rose of ___ (6)
Take one ___ at a time and don't worry about the future (3)
The Grapes of ___ (5)
The Joads had to find work to get it to buy food (5)
The Joads picked them from trees (7)
The Joads went to pick it after peaches (6)
The Rockies, for example (9)
The ___ man told about low wages & starving families (6)
The ___ of Wrath (6)
The banking industry was the ___ that men could not control (7)
There ain't no ___ and there ain't no virtue (3)
They offered their tent to Grandpa (7)
Tom used one to smash the head of one of Casy's attackers (4)
Tons of it were left to rot (5)
Too much rain caused one (5)
While the Joads were stopped to fix it, a man told them about work to the north (4)
Workers at the peach orchard went on ___ for higher wages (6)

Grapes of Wrath Word Search 3

```
B K F R H P P B W Z Y D T J S P D M M K
H Q Z D M O E W X L Q E T F H H Q L O F
Z N M G W N O A J H Y P X L F L N W N K
L J R C V B W V C X Q R N Y N S R R S G
R K L W J H G Z E H J E D R Y O V A T G
L C S O N X W X N R E S M F B H A T E Z
M I G R A N T O M D V S E P A R G H R Z
H O M K G M T M O N H I V M B M S H L S
L Y N R H T V O F A G O L R P Y I W P R
J F W E O X L D R G R N F L E M S L X S
Q V Y C Y F R O T C A R T S E W N W Y L
J A K L C U N P A N N Q A R X I R I T H
D C M T T A B Q I M D C I M S D A L U T
S Q S H F F M M N V M T T M K E G S P C
F T I B A R N P R M A B U L C S G O E J
R E R K V L D E O D Q L R C E E E N D Q
U C B I J D V D F X E P T O B R D S C M
I X R Y K I L S I Y P P L N N T J I M Q
T T C F R E R H L D T Q E N I B G B F T
W P G G I B V N A Y B H M I E J J X R N
R C W F Z S L K C K S X Z E T F O H T X
M M N M T H O M A S F F W G S G R H S X
T I V F Z L V M Q C G W W K M B C Z N M
W M O U N T A I N S C P B G T R X S X M
```

BABY	DEPRESSION	JIM	PA	THOMAS
BARN	DEPUTY	JOHN	PEACHES	TIRE
CALIFORNIA	DESERT	MA	RAGGED	TOM
CAMP	FAMILY	MIGRANT	RIVER	TRACTOR
CLUB	FLOOD	MONEY	RUTHIE	TURTLE
CONNIE	FRUIT	MONSTER	SHARON	WILSONS
COTTON	GRANDMA	MOUNTAINS	SIN	WINFIELD
DAY	GRAPES	MULEY	STEINBECK	WORK
	HOOVERVILLE	NOAH	STRIKE	WRATH

Grapes of Wrath Word Search 3 Answer Key

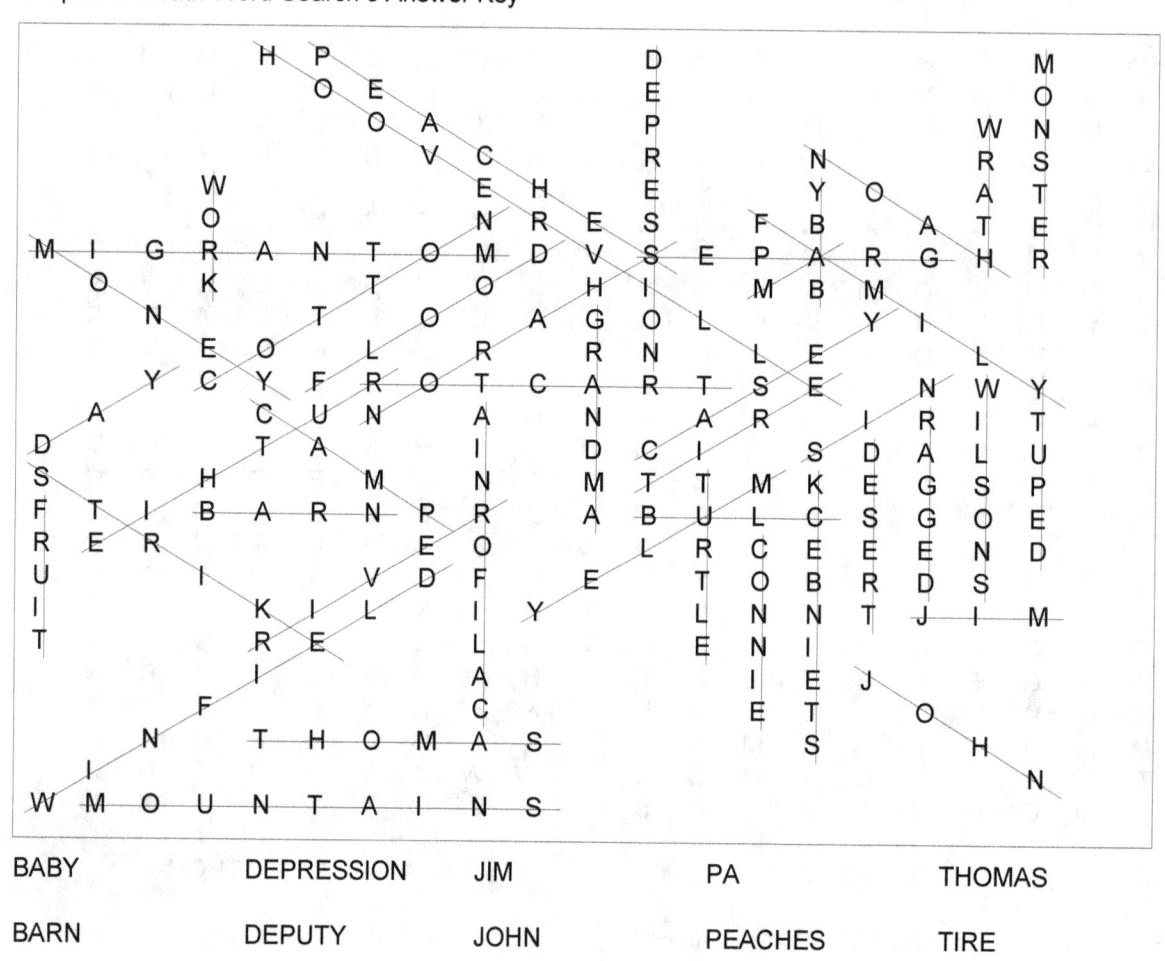

BABY	DEPRESSION	JIM	PA	THOMAS
BARN	DEPUTY	JOHN	PEACHES	TIRE
CALIFORNIA	DESERT	MA	RAGGED	TOM
CAMP	FAMILY	MIGRANT	RIVER	TRACTOR
CLUB	FLOOD	MONEY	RUTHIE	TURTLE
CONNIE	FRUIT	MONSTER	SHARON	WILSONS
COTTON	GRANDMA	MOUNTAINS	SIN	WINFIELD
DAY	GRAPES	MULEY	STEINBECK	WORK
	HOOVERVILLE	NOAH	STRIKE	WRATH

Grapes of Wrath Word Search 4

```
P E A C H E S N O S L I W B R M P F M Z
F X J A A E J H M E H B R I A A A L U R
K J O P L L G O T P R A V D N R X O L T
Y N V T C M I J L A T E R D J F N O E M
X P R R L O R F M R R J E O M L I D Y D
K U U V U N M J O G V G G T N O N E S V
T Q T G B S C I J R G W L R X C N S L C
T W H Z V T K X G A N N J A G J O E R D
F M I Q H E G T R R B I H C S V I R Y D
M J E J D R B S R X A R A T J J S T D R
J P T V A S X P T G P N T O J S S R S L
M F Q N H K G R X E N Q T R F C E X C H
H W D G B B X Q Y D I K T R Y K R W Z H
P M B W T P F J F E R N H H T B P P Z D
A B J C Y S B S M P L N B M O S E M L X
B K V V X V G A D U W K S E N M D C J Y
L N K T M S V V B T N R S I C E A T Y Y
G H F G J Y Q M G Y P M A C N K F S S L
F F D Q A F X R L L Q T O T R I R E L G
W D M D W P N I Z M N N P O H R U Y V Z
C O T T O N M Q K U N M W M F T I R E D
Y B O M L A K J O I Q V I Q H S T M D V
F M T Y F R J M E L W J K S G M X G P B
H O O V E R E V I L L E B V B Z J T L B X
```

BABY	DEPRESSION	JIM	PA	THOMAS
BARN	DEPUTY	JOHN	PEACHES	TIRE
CALIFORNIA	DESERT	MA	RAGGED	TOM
CAMP	FAMILY	MIGRANT	RIVER	TRACTOR
CLUB	FLOOD	MONEY	RUTHIE	TURTLE
CONNIE	FRUIT	MONSTER	SHARON	WILSONS
COTTON	GRANDMA	MOUNTAINS	SIN	WINFIELD
DAY	GRAPES	MULEY	STEINBECK	WORK
	HOOVERVILLE	NOAH	STRIKE	WRATH

Grapes of Wrath Word Search 4 Answer Key

BABY	DEPRESSION	JIM	PA	THOMAS
BARN	DEPUTY	JOHN	PEACHES	TIRE
CALIFORNIA	DESERT	MA	RAGGED	TOM
CAMP	FAMILY	MIGRANT	RIVER	TRACTOR
CLUB	FLOOD	MONEY	RUTHIE	TURTLE
CONNIE	FRUIT	MONSTER	SHARON	WILSONS
COTTON	GRANDMA	MOUNTAINS	SIN	WINFIELD
DAY	GRAPES	MULEY	STEINBECK	WORK
	HOOVERVILLE	NOAH	STRIKE	WRATH

The Grapes of Wrath Crossword 1

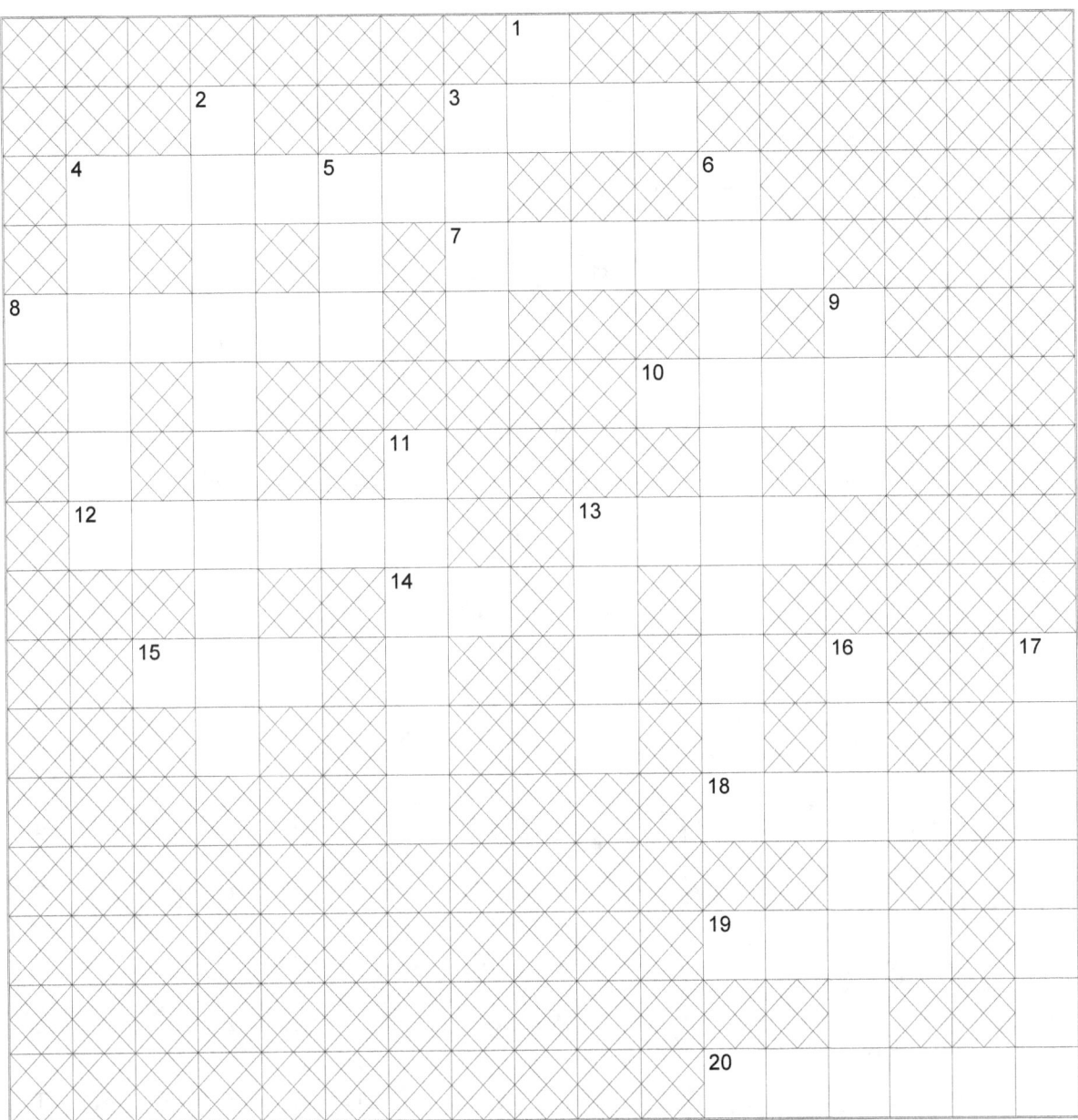

Across
3. It was born dead
4. She died just before the agricultural inspection station
7. The ___ man told about low wages & starving families
8. Ma Joad believed that the ___ should stay together
10. Tons of it were left to rot
12. Workers at the peach orchard went on ___ for higher wages
13. Jim's last name
14. Mr. Joad
15. There ain't no ___ and there ain't no virtue
18. He had a strange sense of calmness about him
19. His wife died from a burst appendix
20. Hot, dry land Joads crossed to get to California

Down
1. Mrs. Joad
2. The Joads' destination
3. Last place of shelter where the Joads found an old man
4. The ___ of Wrath
5. Take one ___ at a time and don't worry about the future
6. Era in American history in which the story is set
9. Former preacher
11. Casy kicked him so Tom could get away
13. Place to pitch a tent and spend the night
16. The Joads picked them from trees
17. Kind of workers who move from place to place

The Grapes of Wrath Crossword 1 Answer Key

Across
- 3. It was born dead
- 4. She died just before the agricultural inspection station
- 7. The ___ man told about low wages & starving families
- 8. Ma Joad believed that the ___ should stay together
- 10. Tons of it were left to rot
- 12. Workers at the peach orchard went on ___ for higher wages
- 13. Jim's last name
- 14. Mr. Joad
- 15. There ain't no ___ and there ain't no virtue
- 18. He had a strange sense of calmness about him
- 19. His wife died from a burst appendix
- 20. Hot, dry land Joads crossed to get to California

Down
- 1. Mrs. Joad
- 2. The Joads' destination
- 3. Last place of shelter where the Joads found an old man
- 4. The ___ of Wrath
- 5. Take one ___ at a time and don't worry about the future
- 6. Era in American history in which the story is set
- 9. Former preacher
- 11. Casy kicked him so Tom could get away
- 13. Place to pitch a tent and spend the night
- 16. The Joads picked them from trees
- 17. Kind of workers who move from place to place

Answers

Across: 3. BABY; 4. GRANDMA; 7. RAGGED; 8. FAMILY; 10. FRUIT; 12. STRIKE; 13. CASY; 14. PA; 15. SIN; 18. NOAH; 19. JOHN; 20. DESERT

Down: 1. MA; 2. CALIFORNIA; 3. BARN; 4. GRAPES; 5. DAY; 6. DEPRESSION; 9. JIM; 11. DEPUTY; 13. CAMP; 16. PEACHES; 17. MIGRANT

The Grapes of Wrath Crossword 2

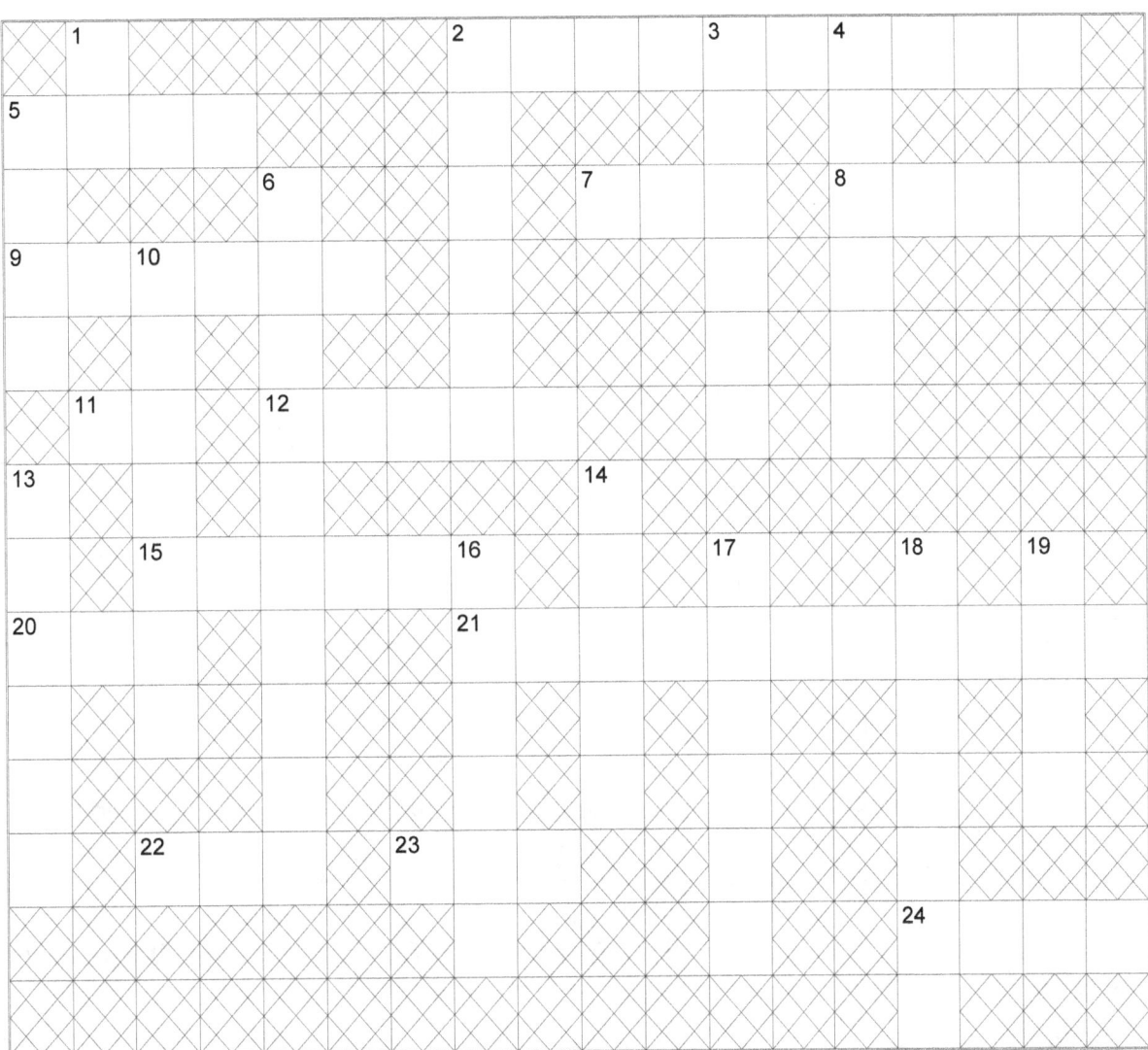

Across
2. The Joads' destination
5. It was born dead
7. Former preacher
8. While the Joads were stopped to fix it, a man told them about work to the north
9. The ___ man told about low wages & starving families
11. Mr. Joad
12. It ran over its banks and flooded the whole area
15. Hot, dry land Joads crossed to get to California
20. He was recently released on parole
21. Nickname for camp for migrant workers
22. There ain't no ___ and there ain't no virtue
23. Take one ___ at a time and don't worry about the future
24. He had a strange sense of calmness about him

Down
1. Mrs. Joad
2. He planned to study a trade but left instead
3. Ma Joad believed that the ___ should stay together
4. She told on Tom
5. Last place of shelter where the Joads found an old man
6. Era in American history in which the story is set
10. She died just before the agricultural inspection station
13. The Joads went to pick it after peaches
14. Too much rain caused one
16. He lowered wages from .30 to .25 per hour
17. Casy kicked him so Tom could get away
18. Kind of workers who move from place to place
19. Tom used one to smash the head of one of Casy's attackers

The Grapes of Wrath Crossword 2 Answer Key

Across
2. The Joads' destination
5. It was born dead
7. Former preacher
8. While the Joads were stopped to fix it, a man told them about work to the north
9. The ___ man told about low wages & starving families
11. Mr. Joad
12. It ran over its banks and flooded the whole area
15. Hot, dry land Joads crossed to get to California
20. He was recently released on parole
21. Nickname for camp for migrant workers
22. There ain't no ___ and there ain't no virtue
23. Take one ___ at a time and don't worry about the future
24. He had a strange sense of calmness about him

Down
1. Mrs. Joad
2. He planned to study a trade but left instead
3. Ma Joad believed that the ___ should stay together
4. She told on Tom
5. Last place of shelter where the Joads found an old man
6. Era in American history in which the story is set
10. She died just before the agricultural inspection station
13. The Joads went to pick it after peaches
14. Too much rain caused one
16. He lowered wages from .30 to .25 per hour
17. Casy kicked him so Tom could get away
18. Kind of workers who move from place to place
19. Tom used one to smash the head of one of Casy's attackers

Answers Grid

Across:
- 2. CALIFORNIA
- 5. BABY
- 7. JIM
- 8. TIRE
- 9. RAGGED
- 11. PA
- 12. RIVER
- 15. DESERT
- 20. TOM
- 21. HOOVERVILLE
- 22. SIN
- 23. DAY
- 24. NOAH

Down:
- 1. MA
- 2. CONNIE
- 3. FAMILY
- 4. RUTHIE
- 5. BARN
- 6. DEPRESSION
- 10. GRAMPA
- 13. COTTON
- 14. FLOOD
- 16. HOLMAN (TOLMOD?)
- 17. DEPUTY
- 18. MIGRANT
- 19. CLUB

The Grapes of Wrath Crossword 3

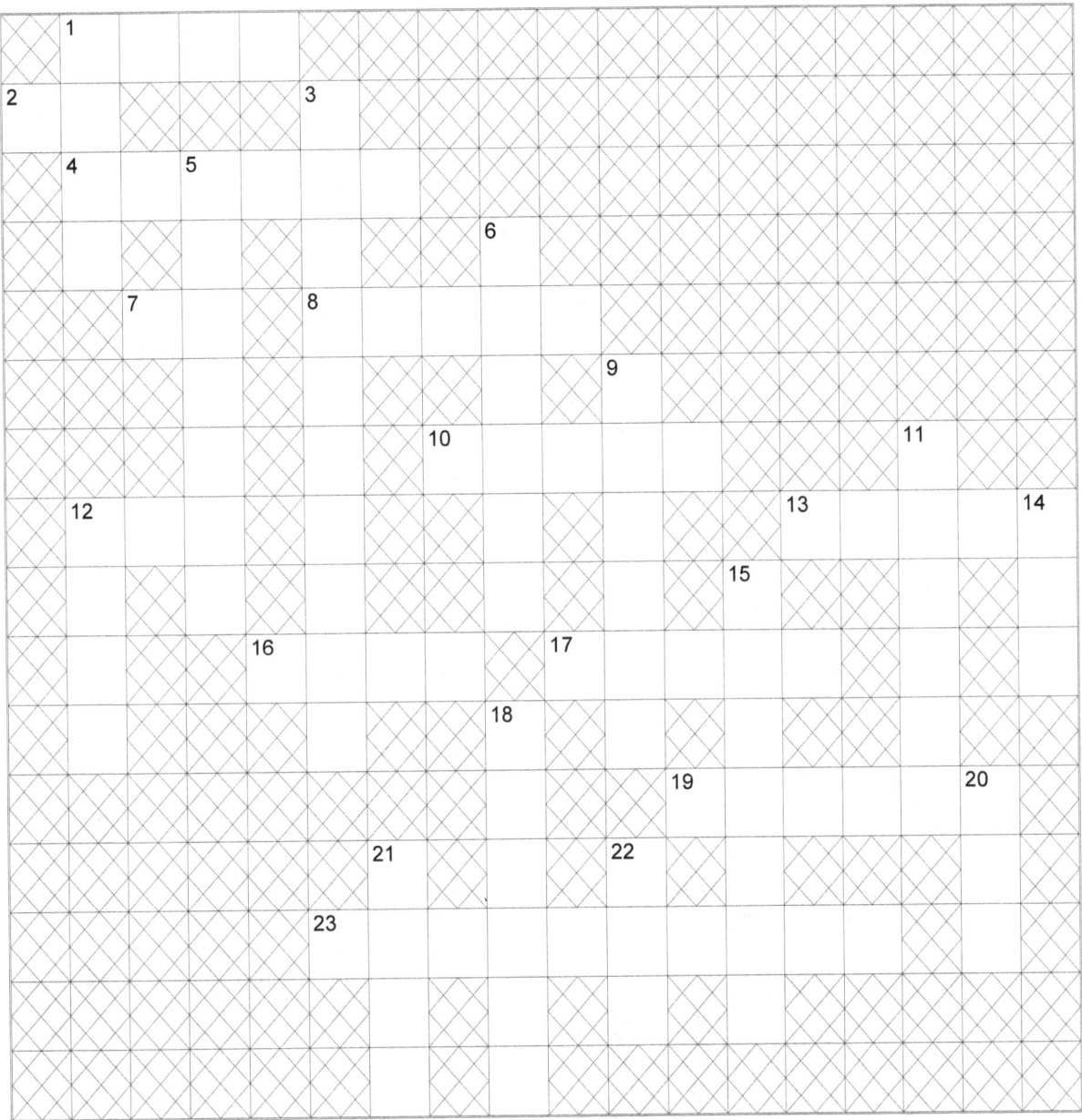

Across
1. It was born dead
2. Mrs. Joad
4. The ___ man told about low wages & starving families
7. Mr. Joad
8. It ran over its banks and flooded the whole area
10. Mr. Graves
12. Former preacher
13. Too much rain caused one
16. He had a strange sense of calmness about him
17. Tons of it were left to rot
19. The ___ of Wrath
23. The Joads' destination

Down
1. Last place of shelter where the Joads found an old man
3. Era in American history in which the story is set
5. She died just before the agricultural inspection station
6. Casy kicked him so Tom could get away
9. Hot, dry land Joads crossed to get to California
11. He planned to study a trade but left instead
12. His wife died from a burst appendix
14. Take one ___ at a time and don't worry about the future
15. Kind of workers who move from place to place
18. Ma Joad believed that the ___ should stay together
20. There ain't no ___ and there ain't no virtue
21. Place to pitch a tent and spend the night
22. He was recently released on parole

The Grapes of Wrath Crossword 3 Answer Key

	¹B	A	B	Y						
²M	A			³D						
	⁴R	A	⁵G	G	E	D				
	N		R		P		⁶D			
		⁷P	A	⁸R	I	V	E	R		
			N		E		P	⁹D		
			D		S	¹⁰M	U	L	E	Y		¹¹C
¹²J	I	M	S		T	S		¹³F	L	O	¹⁴O	D
O		A		I		Y		S		¹⁵M		N	A
H			¹⁶N	O	A	H		¹⁷F	R	U	I	T	Y
N			N			¹⁸F		T		G		I	
						A			¹⁹G	R	A	P	²⁰E	S
			²¹C		²²T		A				I
		²³C	A	L	I	F	O	R	N	I	A	N
			M		L		M		T			
			P		Y							

Across
1. It was born dead
2. Mrs. Joad
4. The ___ man told about low wages & starving families
7. Mr. Joad
8. It ran over its banks and flooded the whole area
10. Mr. Graves
12. Former preacher
13. Too much rain caused one
16. He had a strange sense of calmness about him
17. Tons of it were left to rot
19. The ___ of Wrath
23. The Joads' destination

Down
1. Last place of shelter where the Joads found an old man
3. Era in American history in which the story is set
5. She died just before the agricultural inspection station
6. Casy kicked him so Tom could get away
9. Hot, dry land Joads crossed to get to California
11. He planned to study a trade but left instead
12. His wife died from a burst appendix
14. Take one ___ at a time and don't worry about the future
15. Kind of workers who move from place to place
18. Ma Joad believed that the ___ should stay together
20. There ain't no ___ and there ain't no virtue
21. Place to pitch a tent and spend the night
22. He was recently released on parole

The Grapes of Wrath Crossword 4

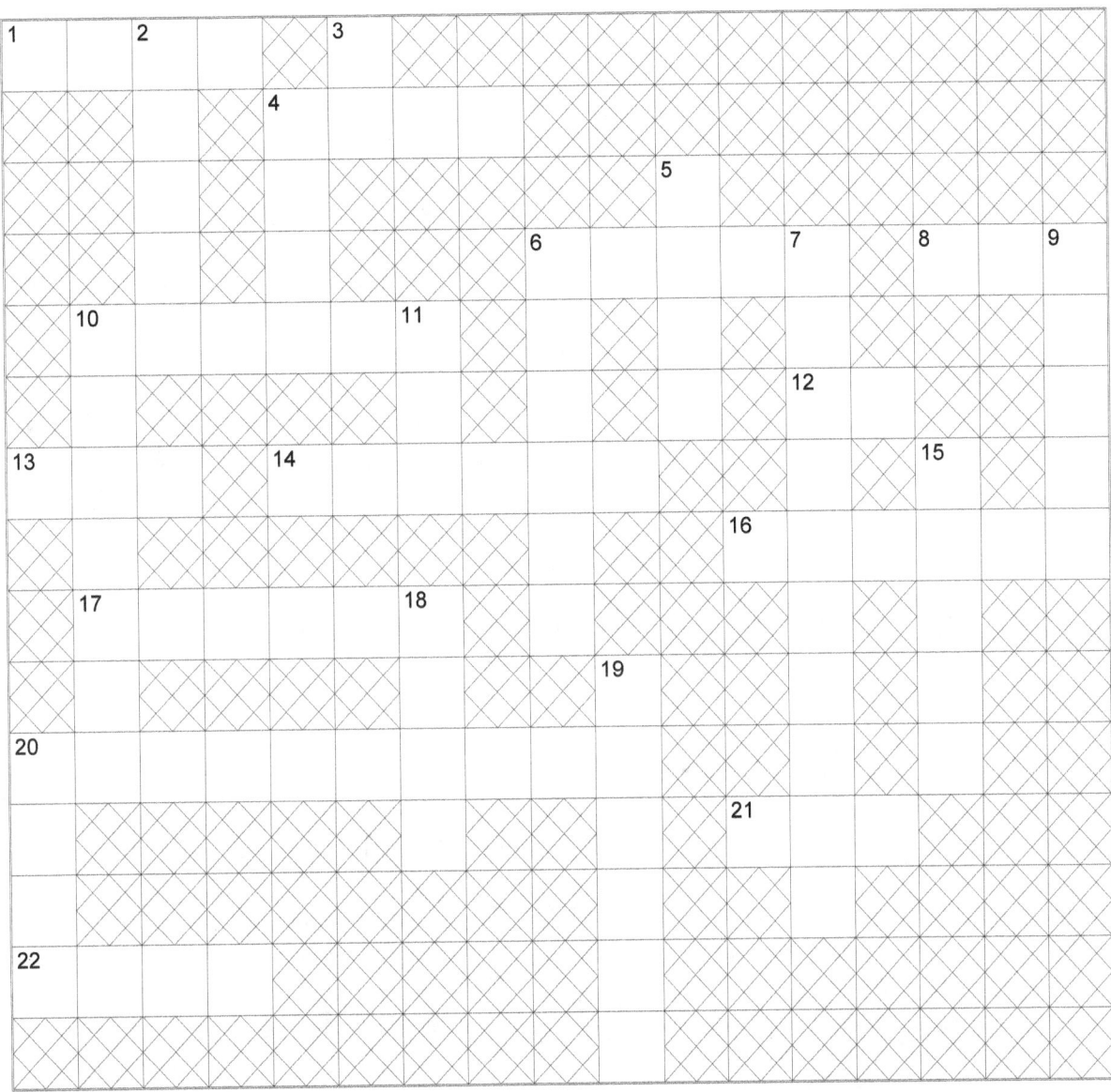

Across
1. Last place of shelter where the Joads found an old man
4. Jim's last name
6. Too much rain caused one
8. Former preacher
10. The ___ of Wrath
12. Mr. Joad
13. Take one ___ at a time and don't worry about the future
14. He planned to study a trade but left instead
16. Casy kicked him so Tom could get away
17. Hot, dry land Joads crossed to get to California
20. The Joads' destination
21. He was recently released on parole
22. It was born dead

Down
2. It ran over its banks and flooded the whole area
3. Mrs. Joad
4. Place to pitch a tent and spend the night
5. His wife died from a burst appendix
6. Ma Joad believed that the ___ should stay together
7. Era in American history in which the story is set
9. The Joads had to find work to get it to buy food
10. She died just before the agricultural inspection station
11. There ain't no ___ and there ain't no virtue
15. Mr. Graves
18. While the Joads were stopped to fix it, a man told them about work to the north
19. The ___ man told about low wages & starving families
20. Tom used one to smash the head of one of Casy's attackers

The Grapes of Wrath Crossword 4 Answer Key

```
 1       2            3
 B   A   R   N        M
             4
         I   C   A   S   Y
                                      5
         V   A                        J
                              6           7       8       9
         E   M                F   L   O   O   D   J   I   M
        10           11
         G   R   A   P   E   S   A   H   E           O
                                              12
         R                I   M   N   P   A       N
        13           14                              15
         D   A   Y       C   O   N   N   I   E       M   E
                                          16
         N                        L       D   E   P   U   T   Y
            17               18
             D   E   S   E   R   T   Y       S       L
                                      19
             M                        I       R       S   E
        20
         C   A   L   I   F   O   R   N   I   A
                                                      21
         L                    E           G       T   O   M
         U                                G           N
        22
         B   A   B   Y                    E
                                          D
```

Across
1. Last place of shelter where the Joads found an old man
4. Jim's last name
6. Too much rain caused one
8. Former preacher
10. The ___ of Wrath
12. Mr. Joad
13. Take one ___ at a time and don't worry about the future
14. He planned to study a trade but left instead
16. Casy kicked him so Tom could get away
17. Hot, dry land Joads crossed to get to California
20. The Joads' destination
21. He was recently released on parole
22. It was born dead

Down
2. It ran over its banks and flooded the whole area
3. Mrs. Joad
4. Place to pitch a tent and spend the night
5. His wife died from a burst appendix
6. Ma Joad believed that the ___ should stay together
7. Era in American history in which the story is set
9. The Joads had to find work to get it to buy food
10. She died just before the agricultural inspection station
11. There ain't no ___ and there ain't no virtue
15. Mr. Graves
18. While the Joads were stopped to fix it, a man told them about work to the north
19. The ___ man told about low wages & starving families
20. Tom used one to smash the head of one of Casy's attackers

The Grapes of Wrath

RUTHIE	RIVER	CLUB	MOUNTAINS	WINFIELD
CALIFORNIA	DEPRESSION	CONNIE	SHARON	TRACTOR
MONEY	PEACHES	FREE SPACE	THOMAS	CAMP
TIRE	FRUIT	JOHN	RAGGED	DEPUTY
GRANDMA	WRATH	SIN	FAMILY	JIM

The Grapes of Wrath

PA	GRAPES	MULEY	MIGRANT	BABY
DAY	COTTON	DESERT	HOOVERVILLE	NOAH
CASY	STEINBECK	FREE SPACE	STRIKE	TOM
FLOOD	TURTLE	WILSONS	WORK	MONSTER
JIM	FAMILY	SIN	WRATH	GRANDMA

The Grapes of Wrath

TURTLE	FAMILY	WRATH	PA	CLUB
CALIFORNIA	GRANDMA	WILSONS	WINFIELD	DESERT
SIN	MULEY	FREE SPACE	COTTON	DAY
SHARON	RAGGED	MONSTER	MONEY	GRAPES
FRUIT	JIM	TRACTOR	RIVER	DEPRESSION

The Grapes of Wrath

JOHN	RUTHIE	MIGRANT	MOUNTAINS	HOOVERVILLE
FLOOD	CAMP	MA	TIRE	TOM
CASY	THOMAS	FREE SPACE	NOAH	STEINBECK
CONNIE	WORK	STRIKE	BARN	BABY
DEPRESSION	RIVER	TRACTOR	JIM	FRUIT

The Grapes of Wrath

DEPUTY	GRAPES	CLUB	FLOOD	DEPRESSION
FRUIT	MONEY	MIGRANT	TRACTOR	PA
CAMP	CONNIE	FREE SPACE	CALIFORNIA	PEACHES
MONSTER	TURTLE	JOHN	WORK	WILSONS
THOMAS	TIRE	MA	HOOVERVILLE	STEINBECK

The Grapes of Wrath

JIM	TOM	SHARON	BARN	NOAH
SIN	BABY	DESERT	WINFIELD	FAMILY
MOUNTAINS	CASY	FREE SPACE	STRIKE	RIVER
MULEY	WRATH	RAGGED	DAY	RUTHIE
STEINBECK	HOOVERVILLE	MA	TIRE	THOMAS

The Grapes of Wrath

SHARON	WINFIELD	CLUB	JOHN	FLOOD
CAMP	MOUNTAINS	MA	TOM	CASY
DAY	WRATH	FREE SPACE	MONSTER	COTTON
TIRE	CALIFORNIA	FRUIT	GRAPES	THOMAS
CONNIE	RAGGED	WORK	DESERT	MONEY

The Grapes of Wrath

SIN	RIVER	NOAH	MULEY	PA
STEINBECK	DEPUTY	JIM	PEACHES	WILSONS
MIGRANT	BABY	FREE SPACE	STRIKE	BARN
TURTLE	FAMILY	RUTHIE	DEPRESSION	TRACTOR
MONEY	DESERT	WORK	RAGGED	CONNIE

The Grapes of Wrath

WRATH	BARN	SIN	WILSONS	THOMAS
CALIFORNIA	DESERT	DEPUTY	MULEY	GRAPES
TURTLE	GRANDMA	FREE SPACE	HOOVERVILLE	RAGGED
CLUB	CONNIE	WINFIELD	WORK	JOHN
STEINBECK	PA	BABY	TIRE	FLOOD

The Grapes of Wrath

MONSTER	RIVER	FAMILY	COTTON	MA
CAMP	MIGRANT	FRUIT	JIM	DAY
DEPRESSION	TRACTOR	FREE SPACE	STRIKE	MOUNTAINS
SHARON	NOAH	CASY	TOM	MONEY
FLOOD	TIRE	BABY	PA	STEINBECK

The Grapes of Wrath

COTTON	MIGRANT	BABY	TRACTOR	NOAH
STEINBECK	WRATH	CASY	MA	FLOOD
DAY	CALIFORNIA	FREE SPACE	SIN	HOOVERVILLE
TURTLE	FAMILY	CLUB	TOM	CAMP
JIM	PA	STRIKE	RAGGED	MOUNTAINS

The Grapes of Wrath

DEPUTY	PEACHES	RIVER	MULEY	GRAPES
WINFIELD	RUTHIE	GRANDMA	TIRE	THOMAS
DEPRESSION	MONSTER	FREE SPACE	BARN	JOHN
DESERT	WILSONS	WORK	CONNIE	MONEY
MOUNTAINS	RAGGED	STRIKE	PA	JIM

The Grapes of Wrath

DESERT	GRAPES	MIGRANT	FAMILY	MONEY
GRANDMA	CALIFORNIA	RUTHIE	STRIKE	DEPRESSION
TRACTOR	FLOOD	FREE SPACE	STEINBECK	JOHN
THOMAS	FRUIT	BABY	TIRE	MOUNTAINS
WINFIELD	RIVER	JIM	SIN	PA

The Grapes of Wrath

SHARON	CASY	CONNIE	WILSONS	MONSTER
RAGGED	COTTON	WORK	DAY	HOOVERVILLE
WRATH	MULEY	FREE SPACE	PEACHES	NOAH
TOM	CLUB	BARN	CAMP	MA
PA	SIN	JIM	RIVER	WINFIELD

The Grapes of Wrath

FRUIT	CALIFORNIA	CLUB	CONNIE	MONSTER
MULEY	MIGRANT	NOAH	CAMP	MOUNTAINS
GRAPES	THOMAS	FREE SPACE	RAGGED	WINFIELD
FAMILY	DEPUTY	TRACTOR	STRIKE	RUTHIE
HOOVERVILLE	TIRE	TURTLE	BABY	MONEY

The Grapes of Wrath

CASY	JIM	FLOOD	PEACHES	DAY
SIN	WORK	COTTON	MA	RIVER
PA	SHARON	FREE SPACE	BARN	WRATH
STEINBECK	TOM	DEPRESSION	JOHN	DESERT
MONEY	BABY	TURTLE	TIRE	HOOVERVILLE

The Grapes of Wrath

GRANDMA	MONEY	THOMAS	MULEY	CALIFORNIA
BABY	DEPUTY	JOHN	WILSONS	TURTLE
FLOOD	CLUB	FREE SPACE	PEACHES	NOAH
MONSTER	COTTON	PA	GRAPES	SIN
TRACTOR	FRUIT	MIGRANT	STRIKE	WORK

The Grapes of Wrath

FAMILY	MOUNTAINS	WRATH	MA	CASY
DAY	DESERT	DEPRESSION	JIM	BARN
TOM	CAMP	FREE SPACE	RAGGED	TIRE
RIVER	STEINBECK	HOOVERVILLE	CONNIE	SHARON
WORK	STRIKE	MIGRANT	FRUIT	TRACTOR

The Grapes of Wrath

WORK	DAY	CLUB	TRACTOR	FRUIT
FLOOD	WRATH	DEPUTY	MA	MIGRANT
COTTON	CASY	FREE SPACE	CONNIE	TURTLE
MONSTER	GRANDMA	PEACHES	THOMAS	BABY
MONEY	TOM	STEINBECK	CAMP	TIRE

The Grapes of Wrath

NOAH	SIN	DEPRESSION	RIVER	BARN
FAMILY	HOOVERVILLE	DESERT	GRAPES	JIM
WILSONS	SHARON	FREE SPACE	MOUNTAINS	RAGGED
JOHN	WINFIELD	MULEY	CALIFORNIA	RUTHIE
TIRE	CAMP	STEINBECK	TOM	MONEY

The Grapes of Wrath

FAMILY	RUTHIE	DAY	TOM	NOAH
GRANDMA	WORK	CALIFORNIA	STRIKE	CONNIE
DEPUTY	SHARON	FREE SPACE	BABY	DEPRESSION
MIGRANT	RIVER	FRUIT	WRATH	THOMAS
CASY	MONEY	WINFIELD	TURTLE	BARN

The Grapes of Wrath

TIRE	JIM	FLOOD	MA	GRAPES
STEINBECK	MONSTER	SIN	JOHN	DESERT
WILSONS	CAMP	FREE SPACE	MULEY	HOOVERVILLE
RAGGED	MOUNTAINS	CLUB	COTTON	TRACTOR
BARN	TURTLE	WINFIELD	MONEY	CASY

The Grapes of Wrath

CALIFORNIA	BARN	JIM	SHARON	MA
MONEY	MULEY	MIGRANT	DESERT	DAY
STRIKE	TRACTOR	FREE SPACE	HOOVERVILLE	DEPRESSION
WORK	GRANDMA	RUTHIE	FLOOD	TURTLE
FRUIT	TOM	DEPUTY	JOHN	NOAH

The Grapes of Wrath

PA	WINFIELD	BABY	CONNIE	RIVER
STEINBECK	TIRE	RAGGED	CLUB	COTTON
GRAPES	SIN	FREE SPACE	MONSTER	MOUNTAINS
FAMILY	WILSONS	CASEY	CAMP	THOMAS
NOAH	JOHN	DEPUTY	TOM	FRUIT

The Grapes of Wrath

JOHN	MONEY	COTTON	DAY	JIM
DESERT	RAGGED	GRANDMA	FAMILY	TURTLE
WINFIELD	GRAPES	FREE SPACE	MA	SHARON
STRIKE	WILSONS	WORK	MULEY	TRACTOR
DEPRESSION	PA	TOM	WRATH	RIVER

The Grapes of Wrath

FRUIT	PEACHES	CONNIE	CLUB	BARN
STEINBECK	THOMAS	SIN	MOUNTAINS	NOAH
TIRE	MIGRANT	FREE SPACE	MONSTER	RUTHIE
BABY	CAMP	DEPUTY	CASY	CALIFORNIA
RIVER	WRATH	TOM	PA	DEPRESSION

The Grapes of Wrath

WRATH	DESERT	BARN	WINFIELD	MONEY
GRANDMA	WILSONS	DAY	TURTLE	MONSTER
HOOVERVILLE	GRAPES	FREE SPACE	TIRE	JIM
CASY	RIVER	SIN	CALIFORNIA	RUTHIE
CLUB	RAGGED	FAMILY	WORK	PA

The Grapes of Wrath

JOHN	DEPRESSION	MOUNTAINS	TRACTOR	COTTON
CONNIE	NOAH	STRIKE	STEINBECK	THOMAS
CAMP	MA	FREE SPACE	SHARON	MULEY
MIGRANT	BABY	FLOOD	DEPUTY	FRUIT
PA	WORK	FAMILY	RAGGED	CLUB

The Grapes of Wrath

RAGGED	JIM	STEINBECK	FAMILY	MIGRANT
CLUB	WINFIELD	WORK	DAY	PA
RIVER	CONNIE	FREE SPACE	DESERT	HOOVERVILLE
BABY	CAMP	MA	GRAPES	RUTHIE
CALIFORNIA	SHARON	WILSONS	SIN	STRIKE

The Grapes of Wrath

BARN	FLOOD	COTTON	DEPUTY	PEACHES
MOUNTAINS	CASY	MONEY	MONSTER	TOM
TIRE	TURTLE	FREE SPACE	TRACTOR	WRATH
THOMAS	JOHN	NOAH	GRANDMA	FRUIT
STRIKE	SIN	WILSONS	SHARON	CALIFORNIA

The Grapes of Wrath

SHARON	CONNIE	BABY	MONEY	BARN
JIM	WINFIELD	FRUIT	COTTON	PEACHES
STEINBECK	CAMP	FREE SPACE	HOOVERVILLE	NOAH
MA	DESERT	WRATH	MONSTER	TURTLE
GRANDMA	STRIKE	MULEY	DEPUTY	CALIFORNIA

The Grapes of Wrath

FLOOD	THOMAS	DAY	WORK	TOM
FAMILY	WILSONS	RUTHIE	MOUNTAINS	TIRE
PA	DEPRESSION	FREE SPACE	TRACTOR	RAGGED
JOHN	SIN	CLUB	GRAPES	CASY
CALIFORNIA	DEPUTY	MULEY	STRIKE	GRANDMA

The Grapes of Wrath Vocabulary Word List

No.	Word	Clue/Definition
1.	ACCOUTERMENTS	Accessories
2.	AGITATORS	People who stir up trouble
3.	ALOOF	Reserved; distant
4.	ANLAGE	Initial cell structure from which a part or organ develops; foundation
5.	APPREHENSION	Anxiousness
6.	ASSAILED	Assaulted
7.	BESEECH	Make an earnest request
8.	CANTANKEROUS	Ill-tempered; difficult to handle
9.	CONCESSION	Compromise
10.	CONQUEST	Accomplishment; having overcome something
11.	CONSERVED	Saved; used sparingly
12.	CONTRITE	Sorry
13.	CULVERT	Drainage ditch
14.	CYNICAL	Scornful of the motives, virtue or integrity of others
15.	DECLIVITY	Slope; hill
16.	DEFIANTLY	In a manner rejecting authority
17.	DEMURE	Shy; modest; reserved
18.	DENUNCIATION	Public condemnation
19.	DISCONSOLATE	Dejected; gloomy
20.	EMERGED	Came out
21.	ENGAGINGLY	Charmingly; attractively
22.	ENGULFED	Swallowed up; surrounded; enclosed
23.	ENSNARED	Caught
24.	EXHORTATION	Speech intended to advise, incite or encourage
25.	FATUOUSLY	Smugly
26.	FERAL	Wild; savage
27.	FETID	Stinky; smelly
28.	FORLORN	Sad because of being abandoned
29.	FRET	Worry
30.	HYPOCRITE	One who says he believes one way but in action shows he believes the opposite
31.	IMPERIOUSLY	Authoritatively
32.	IMPERTURBABLE	Can't be upset or annoyed
33.	INQUIRINGLY	Questioningly
34.	INSIGNIA	Emblem
35.	IRRITABLY	In a manner showing annoyance
36.	LECHEROUS	Tending towards excessive promiscuous behavior
37.	LINGERED	Remained; tarried
38.	LITHELY	Gracefully
39.	LUSTERLESS	Dull
40.	LUXURIOUSLY	As an indulgence; not necessarily out of necessity
41.	MENACINGLY	Threateningly
42.	MINCING	Walking with short steps
43.	MODULATED	With a varying tone
44.	NEBULOUS	Lacking definite form
45.	NONDESCRIPT	Having no individual, distinguishing characteristics
46.	OBLIGATION	Duty; contract; promise
47.	OBSCURED	Hidden from view
48.	OSTRACISM	Being shunned or ignored by the group
49.	PALL	Gloomy atmosphere
50.	PANORAMIC	With a wide view
51.	PARADOXES	Seemingly contradictory aspects
52.	PERPLEXITY	Confusion; puzzlement

The Grapes of Wrath Vocabulary Word List Continued

No. Word	Clue/Definition
53. PINNACLES	Tall, pointed formations
54. PRECINCT	District
55. PRECIOUS	Valuable
56. PRODIGAL	Extravagant
57. PROPRIETOR	Owner
58. PROVOCATIVELY	In an exciting or stimulating way
59. PUTRESCENCE	Rotten, decaying matter
60. RAVENOUS	Extremely hungry
61. REASSURED	Restored confidence
62. RECEDED	Withdrew
63. SAUNTERED	Strolled
64. SERENE	Calm, peaceful
65. SKULK	Lurk; lie in hiding
66. SULKILY	Gloomily; in a withdrawn manner
67. TAUT	Tight; tense
68. TIMBRE	Distinguishing quality of a sound
69. TRUCULENTLY	Fiercely
70. VAGUE	Not clearly expressive
71. VITALITY	Energy; liveliness
72. VIVACIOUSNESS	Liveliness; animation
73. WIZENED	Withered; wrinkled

The Grapes of Wrath Vocabulary Fill In The Blank 1

_____ 1. Questioningly

_____ 2. Withered; wrinkled

_____ 3. Extremely hungry

_____ 4. Accessories

_____ 5. Lurk; lie in hiding

_____ 6. Reserved; distant

_____ 7. Distinguishing quality of a sound

_____ 8. Valuable

_____ 9. Worry

_____ 10. Slope; hill

_____ 11. Gloomy atmosphere

_____ 12. Came out

_____ 13. Ill-tempered; difficult to handle

_____ 14. Lacking definite form

_____ 15. Dejected; gloomy

_____ 16. Seemingly contradictory aspects

_____ 17. With a wide view

_____ 18. One who says he believes one way but in action shows he believes the opposite

_____ 19. Duty; contract; promise

_____ 20. Tight; tense

The Grapes of Wrath Vocabulary Fill In The Blank 1 Answer Key

INQUIRINGLY	1. Questioningly
WIZENED	2. Withered; wrinkled
RAVENOUS	3. Extremely hungry
ACCOUTERMENTS	4. Accessories
SKULK	5. Lurk; lie in hiding
ALOOF	6. Reserved; distant
TIMBRE	7. Distinguishing quality of a sound
PRECIOUS	8. Valuable
FRET	9. Worry
DECLIVITY	10. Slope; hill
PALL	11. Gloomy atmosphere
EMERGED	12. Came out
CANTANKEROUS	13. Ill-tempered; difficult to handle
NEBULOUS	14. Lacking definite form
DISCONSOLATE	15. Dejected; gloomy
PARADOXES	16. Seemingly contradictory aspects
PANORAMIC	17. With a wide view
HYPOCRITE	18. One who says he believes one way but in action shows he believes the opposite
OBLIGATION	19. Duty; contract; promise
TAUT	20. Tight; tense

The Grapes of Wrath Vocabulary Fill In The Blank 2

_____ 1. Rotten, decaying matter

_____ 2. Gracefully

_____ 3. Emblem

_____ 4. Accessories

_____ 5. Confusion; puzzlement

_____ 6. Sad because of being abandoned

_____ 7. Not clearly expressive

_____ 8. Anxiousness

_____ 9. One who says he believes one way but in action shows he believes the opposite

_____ 10. Energy; liveliness

_____ 11. Slope; hill

_____ 12. Distinguishing quality of a sound

_____ 13. In a manner showing annoyance

_____ 14. Drainage ditch

_____ 15. With a wide view

_____ 16. Wild; savage

_____ 17. Public condemnation

_____ 18. Dejected; gloomy

_____ 19. Withdrew

_____ 20. Valuable

The Grapes of Wrath Vocabulary Fill In The Blank 2 Answer Key

PUTRESCENCE	1. Rotten, decaying matter
LITHELY	2. Gracefully
INSIGNIA	3. Emblem
ACCOUTERMENTS	4. Accessories
PERPLEXITY	5. Confusion; puzzlement
FORLORN	6. Sad because of being abandoned
VAGUE	7. Not clearly expressive
APPREHENSION	8. Anxiousness
HYPOCRITE	9. One who says he believes one way but in action shows he believes the opposite
VITALITY	10. Energy; liveliness
DECLIVITY	11. Slope; hill
TIMBRE	12. Distinguishing quality of a sound
IRRITABLY	13. In a manner showing annoyance
CULVERT	14. Drainage ditch
PANORAMIC	15. With a wide view
FERAL	16. Wild; savage
DENUNCIATION	17. Public condemnation
DISCONSOLATE	18. Dejected; gloomy
RECEDED	19. Withdrew
PRECIOUS	20. Valuable

The Grapes of Wrath Vocabulary Fill In The Blank 3

1. Compromise
2. Liveliness; animation
3. Slope; hill
4. Gracefully
5. Anxiousness
6. Duty; contract; promise
7. Lurk; lie in hiding
8. Can't be upset or annoyed
9. Assaulted
10. Sorry
11. Owner
12. Scornful of the motives, virtue or integrity of others
13. Stinky; smelly
14. Walking with short steps
15. Tending towards excessive promiscuous behavior
16. Seemingly contradictory aspects
17. Threateningly
18. Wild; savage
19. Make an earnest request
20. Energy; liveliness

The Grapes of Wrath Vocabulary Fill In The Blank 3 Answer Key

CONCESSION	1. Compromise
VIVACIOUSNESS	2. Liveliness; animation
DECLIVITY	3. Slope; hill
LITHELY	4. Gracefully
APPREHENSION	5. Anxiousness
OBLIGATION	6. Duty; contract; promise
SKULK	7. Lurk; lie in hiding
IMPERTURBABLE	8. Can't be upset or annoyed
ASSAILED	9. Assaulted
CONTRITE	10. Sorry
PROPRIETOR	11. Owner
CYNICAL	12. Scornful of the motives, virtue or integrity of others
FETID	13. Stinky; smelly
MINCING	14. Walking with short steps
LECHEROUS	15. Tending towards excessive promiscuous behavior
PARADOXES	16. Seemingly contradictory aspects
MENACINGLY	17. Threateningly
FERAL	18. Wild; savage
BESEECH	19. Make an earnest request
VITALITY	20. Energy; liveliness

The Grapes of Wrath Vocabulary Fill In The Blank 4

_____ 1. Caught

_____ 2. Accomplishment; having overcome something

_____ 3. Withdrew

_____ 4. Seemingly contradictory aspects

_____ 5. Gracefully

_____ 6. Swallowed up; surrounded; enclosed

_____ 7. Anxiousness

_____ 8. Gloomy atmosphere

_____ 9. Drainage ditch

_____ 10. Questioningly

_____ 11. Charmingly; attractively

_____ 12. Ill-tempered; difficult to handle

_____ 13. Hidden from view

_____ 14. Having no individual, distinguishing characteristics

_____ 15. Extremely hungry

_____ 16. Dejected; gloomy

_____ 17. Shy; modest; reserved

_____ 18. Duty; contract; promise

_____ 19. As an indulgence; not necessarily out of necessity

_____ 20. Stinky; smelly

The Grapes of Wrath Vocabulary Fill In The Blank 4 Answer Key

ENSNARED	1. Caught
CONQUEST	2. Accomplishment; having overcome something
RECEDED	3. Withdrew
PARADOXES	4. Seemingly contradictory aspects
LITHELY	5. Gracefully
ENGULFED	6. Swallowed up; surrounded; enclosed
APPREHENSION	7. Anxiousness
PALL	8. Gloomy atmosphere
CULVERT	9. Drainage ditch
INQUIRINGLY	10. Questioningly
ENGAGINGLY	11. Charmingly; attractively
CANTANKEROUS	12. Ill-tempered; difficult to handle
OBSCURED	13. Hidden from view
NONDESCRIPT	14. Having no individual, distinguishing characteristics
RAVENOUS	15. Extremely hungry
DISCONSOLATE	16. Dejected; gloomy
DEMURE	17. Shy; modest; reserved
OBLIGATION	18. Duty; contract; promise
LUXURIOUSLY	19. As an indulgence; not necessarily out of necessity
FETID	20. Stinky; smelly

The Grapes of Wrath Vocabulary Matching 1

___ 1. DISCONSOLATE   A. Slope; hill
___ 2. SKULK   B. Tall, pointed formations
___ 3. LUXURIOUSLY   C. Saved; used sparingly
___ 4. OBSCURED   D. Came out
___ 5. SULKILY   E. Owner
___ 6. SERENE   F. Valuable
___ 7. REASSURED   G. Sorry
___ 8. DECLIVITY   H. Accomplishment; having overcome something
___ 9. PROVOCATIVELY   I. With a varying tone
___ 10. FRET   J. Tight; tense
___ 11. PUTRESCENCE   K. Extremely hungry
___ 12. RAVENOUS   L. Gloomily; in a withdrawn manner
___ 13. OSTRACISM   M. Calm, peaceful
___ 14. ENGAGINGLY   N. Charmingly; attractively
___ 15. EMERGED   O. In an exciting or stimulating way
___ 16. CONQUEST   P. Rotten, decaying matter
___ 17. IMPERIOUSLY   Q. Worry
___ 18. MODULATED   R. Being shunned or ignored by the group
___ 19. TAUT   S. In a manner rejecting authority
___ 20. CONTRITE   T. Restored confidence
___ 21. PRECIOUS   U. Authoritatively
___ 22. CONSERVED   V. Hidden from view
___ 23. PROPRIETOR   W. Dejected; gloomy
___ 24. PINNACLES   X. Lurk; lie in hiding
___ 25. DEFIANTLY   Y. As an indulgence; not necessarily out of necessity

The Grapes of Wrath Vocabulary Matching 1 Answer Key

W - 1. DISCONSOLATE		A. Slope; hill
X - 2. SKULK		B. Tall, pointed formations
Y - 3. LUXURIOUSLY		C. Saved; used sparingly
V - 4. OBSCURED		D. Came out
L - 5. SULKILY		E. Owner
M - 6. SERENE		F. Valuable
T - 7. REASSURED		G. Sorry
A - 8. DECLIVITY		H. Accomplishment; having overcome something
O - 9. PROVOCATIVELY		I. With a varying tone
Q - 10. FRET		J. Tight; tense
P - 11. PUTRESCENCE		K. Extremely hungry
K - 12. RAVENOUS		L. Gloomily; in a withdrawn manner
R - 13. OSTRACISM		M. Calm, peaceful
N - 14. ENGAGINGLY		N. Charmingly; attractively
D - 15. EMERGED		O. In an exciting or stimulating way
H - 16. CONQUEST		P. Rotten, decaying matter
U - 17. IMPERIOUSLY		Q. Worry
I - 18. MODULATED		R. Being shunned or ignored by the group
J - 19. TAUT		S. In a manner rejecting authority
G - 20. CONTRITE		T. Restored confidence
F - 21. PRECIOUS		U. Authoritatively
C - 22. CONSERVED		V. Hidden from view
E - 23. PROPRIETOR		W. Dejected; gloomy
B - 24. PINNACLES		X. Lurk; lie in hiding
S - 25. DEFIANTLY		Y. As an indulgence; not necessarily out of necessity

Copyrighted

The Grapes of Wrath Vocabulary Matching 2

___ 1. ANLAGE
___ 2. AGITATORS
___ 3. IMPERTURBABLE
___ 4. OBLIGATION
___ 5. PRECINCT
___ 6. ASSAILED
___ 7. IRRITABLY
___ 8. DENUNCIATION
___ 9. SERENE
___ 10. PANORAMIC
___ 11. MENACINGLY
___ 12. DEMURE
___ 13. PALL
___ 14. CULVERT
___ 15. PUTRESCENCE
___ 16. LUXURIOUSLY
___ 17. PRODIGAL
___ 18. FATUOUSLY
___ 19. IMPERIOUSLY
___ 20. TAUT
___ 21. CONQUEST
___ 22. MINCING
___ 23. ENSNARED
___ 24. RAVENOUS
___ 25. LITHELY

A. Gloomy atmosphere
B. Assaulted
C. Public condemnation
D. Shy; modest; reserved
E. Caught
F. Accomplishment; having overcome something
G. Authoritatively
H. Walking with short steps
I. Rotten, decaying matter
J. Calm, peaceful
K. Initial cell structure from which a part or organ develops; foundation
L. In a manner showing annoyance
M. With a wide view
N. Can't be upset or annoyed
O. Duty; contract; promise
P. Tight; tense
Q. District
R. People who stir up trouble
S. Smugly
T. Drainage ditch
U. Extravagant
V. Gracefully
W. Threateningly
X. As an indulgence; not necessarily out of necessity
Y. Extremely hungry

The Grapes of Wrath Vocabulary Matching 2 Answer Key

K - 1. ANLAGE		A. Gloomy atmosphere
R - 2. AGITATORS		B. Assaulted
N - 3. IMPERTURBABLE		C. Public condemnation
O - 4. OBLIGATION		D. Shy; modest; reserved
Q - 5. PRECINCT		E. Caught
B - 6. ASSAILED		F. Accomplishment; having overcome something
L - 7. IRRITABLY		G. Authoritatively
C - 8. DENUNCIATION		H. Walking with short steps
J - 9. SERENE		I. Rotten, decaying matter
M - 10. PANORAMIC		J. Calm, peaceful
W - 11. MENACINGLY		K. Initial cell structure from which a part or organ develops; foundation
D - 12. DEMURE		L. In a manner showing annoyance
A - 13. PALL		M. With a wide view
T - 14. CULVERT		N. Can't be upset or annoyed
I - 15. PUTRESCENCE		O. Duty; contract; promise
X - 16. LUXURIOUSLY		P. Tight; tense
U - 17. PRODIGAL		Q. District
S - 18. FATUOUSLY		R. People who stir up trouble
G - 19. IMPERIOUSLY		S. Smugly
P - 20. TAUT		T. Drainage ditch
F - 21. CONQUEST		U. Extravagant
H - 22. MINCING		V. Gracefully
E - 23. ENSNARED		W. Threateningly
Y - 24. RAVENOUS		X. As an indulgence; not necessarily out of necessity
V - 25. LITHELY		Y. Extremely hungry

The Grapes of Wrath Vocabulary Matching 3

___ 1. LECHEROUS   A. Liveliness; animation
___ 2. FRET   B. Sorry
___ 3. OSTRACISM   C. Can't be upset or annoyed
___ 4. ENSNARED   D. Rotten, decaying matter
___ 5. REASSURED   E. Scornful of the motives, virtue or integrity of others
___ 6. MENACINGLY   F. Lurk; lie in hiding
___ 7. ACCOUTERMENTS   G. Slope; hill
___ 8. VIVACIOUSNESS   H. Confusion; puzzlement
___ 9. WIZENED   I. Gloomily; in a withdrawn manner
___10. PERPLEXITY   J. Owner
___11. CYNICAL   K. Walking with short steps
___12. SKULK   L. Extremely hungry
___13. INQUIRINGLY   M. Valuable
___14. DISCONSOLATE   N. Restored confidence
___15. DECLIVITY   O. Reserved; distant
___16. ALOOF   P. Being shunned or ignored by the group
___17. IMPERTURBABLE   Q. Tending towards excessive promiscuous behavior
___18. SULKILY   R. Questioningly
___19. MINCING   S. Accessories
___20. SERENE   T. Dejected; gloomy
___21. PROPRIETOR   U. Withered; wrinkled
___22. PRECIOUS   V. Calm, peaceful
___23. RAVENOUS   W. Caught
___24. CONTRITE   X. Worry
___25. PUTRESCENCE   Y. Threateningly

The Grapes of Wrath Vocabulary Matching 3 Answer Key

Q - 1.	LECHEROUS	A. Liveliness; animation
X - 2.	FRET	B. Sorry
P - 3.	OSTRACISM	C. Can't be upset or annoyed
W - 4.	ENSNARED	D. Rotten, decaying matter
N - 5.	REASSURED	E. Scornful of the motives, virtue or integrity of others
Y - 6.	MENACINGLY	F. Lurk; lie in hiding
S - 7.	ACCOUTERMENTS	G. Slope; hill
A - 8.	VIVACIOUSNESS	H. Confusion; puzzlement
U - 9.	WIZENED	I. Gloomily; in a withdrawn manner
H - 10.	PERPLEXITY	J. Owner
E - 11.	CYNICAL	K. Walking with short steps
F - 12.	SKULK	L. Extremely hungry
R - 13.	INQUIRINGLY	M. Valuable
T - 14.	DISCONSOLATE	N. Restored confidence
G - 15.	DECLIVITY	O. Reserved; distant
O - 16.	ALOOF	P. Being shunned or ignored by the group
C - 17.	IMPERTURBABLE	Q. Tending towards excessive promiscuous behavior
I - 18.	SULKILY	R. Questioningly
K - 19.	MINCING	S. Accessories
V - 20.	SERENE	T. Dejected; gloomy
J - 21.	PROPRIETOR	U. Withered; wrinkled
M - 22.	PRECIOUS	V. Calm, peaceful
L - 23.	RAVENOUS	W. Caught
B - 24.	CONTRITE	X. Worry
D - 25.	PUTRESCENCE	Y. Threateningly

The Grapes of Wrath Vocabulary Matching 4

___ 1. RECEDED
___ 2. CONQUEST
___ 3. FRET
___ 4. LUSTERLESS
___ 5. TIMBRE
___ 6. PERPLEXITY
___ 7. CANTANKEROUS
___ 8. OBLIGATION
___ 9. OSTRACISM
___ 10. INSIGNIA
___ 11. INQUIRINGLY
___ 12. AGITATORS
___ 13. DISCONSOLATE
___ 14. TAUT
___ 15. EXHORTATION
___ 16. PINNACLES
___ 17. CONTRITE
___ 18. OBSCURED
___ 19. IMPERTURBABLE
___ 20. DEFIANTLY
___ 21. ACCOUTERMENTS
___ 22. CYNICAL
___ 23. DEMURE
___ 24. FATUOUSLY
___ 25. ASSAILED

A. Shy; modest; reserved
B. Distinguishing quality of a sound
C. Tight; tense
D. Worry
E. Being shunned or ignored by the group
F. Dull
G. Speech intended to advise, incite or encourage
H. Hidden from view
I. Scornful of the motives, virtue or integrity of others
J. Ill-tempered; difficult to handle
K. Accessories
L. People who stir up trouble
M. Tall, pointed formations
N. Accomplishment; having overcome something
O. Smugly
P. Confusion; puzzlement
Q. Questioningly
R. In a manner rejecting authority
S. Assaulted
T. Withdrew
U. Dejected; gloomy
V. Sorry
W. Can't be upset or annoyed
X. Duty; contract; promise
Y. Emblem

The Grapes of Wrath Vocabulary Matching 4 Answer Key

T - 1. RECEDED		A. Shy; modest; reserved
N - 2. CONQUEST		B. Distinguishing quality of a sound
D - 3. FRET		C. Tight; tense
F - 4. LUSTERLESS		D. Worry
B - 5. TIMBRE		E. Being shunned or ignored by the group
P - 6. PERPLEXITY		F. Dull
J - 7. CANTANKEROUS		G. Speech intended to advise, incite or encourage
X - 8. OBLIGATION		H. Hidden from view
E - 9. OSTRACISM		I. Scornful of the motives, virtue or integrity of others
Y -10. INSIGNIA		J. Ill-tempered; difficult to handle
Q -11. INQUIRINGLY		K. Accessories
L -12. AGITATORS		L. People who stir up trouble
U -13. DISCONSOLATE		M. Tall, pointed formations
C -14. TAUT		N. Accomplishment; having overcome something
G -15. EXHORTATION		O. Smugly
M -16. PINNACLES		P. Confusion; puzzlement
V -17. CONTRITE		Q. Questioningly
H -18. OBSCURED		R. In a manner rejecting authority
W -19. IMPERTURBABLE		S. Assaulted
R -20. DEFIANTLY		T. Withdrew
K -21. ACCOUTERMENTS		U. Dejected; gloomy
I - 22. CYNICAL		V. Sorry
A -23. DEMURE		W. Can't be upset or annoyed
O -24. FATUOUSLY		X. Duty; contract; promise
S -25. ASSAILED		Y. Emblem

The Grapes of Wrath Vocabulary Magic Squares 1

Match the definition with the vocabulary word. Put your answers in the magic squares below. When your answers are correct, all columns and rows will add to the same number.

A. PRODIGAL
B. FATUOUSLY
C. LINGERED
D. FETID
E. EXHORTATION
F. CONSERVED
G. TRUCULENTLY
H. SULKILY
I. ANLAGE
J. PROVOCATIVELY
K. DISCONSOLATE
L. PERPLEXITY
M. TAUT
N. OSTRACISM
O. HYPOCRITE
P. LUXURIOUSLY

1. Gloomily; in a withdrawn manner
2. Extravagant
3. Smugly
4. Fiercely
5. In an exciting or stimulating way
6. One who says he believes one way but in action shows he believes the opposite
7. As an indulgence; not necessarily out of necessity
8. Initial cell structure from which a part or organ develops; foundation
9. Dejected; gloomy
10. Being shunned or ignored by the group
11. Tight; tense
12. Confusion; puzzlement
13. Speech intended to advise, incite or encourage
14. Stinky; smelly
15. Remained; tarried
16. Saved; used sparingly

A=	B=	C=	D=
E=	F=	G=	H=
I=	J=	K=	L=
M=	N=	O=	P=

The Grapes of Wrath Vocabulary Magic Squares 1 Answer Key

Match the definition with the vocabulary word. Put your answers in the magic squares below. When your answers are correct, all columns and rows will add to the same number.

A. PRODIGAL
B. FATUOUSLY
C. LINGERED
D. FETID
E. EXHORTATION
F. CONSERVED
G. TRUCULENTLY
H. SULKILY
I. ANLAGE
J. PROVOCATIVELY
K. DISCONSOLATE
L. PERPLEXITY
M. TAUT
N. OSTRACISM
O. HYPOCRITE
P. LUXURIOUSLY

1. Gloomily; in a withdrawn manner
2. Extravagant
3. Smugly
4. Fiercely
5. In an exciting or stimulating way
6. One who says he believes one way but in action shows he believes the opposite
7. As an indulgence;not necessarily out of necessity
8. Initial cell structure from which a part or organ develops; foundation
9. Dejected; gloomy
10. Being shunned or ignored by the group
11. Tight; tense
12. Confusion; puzzlement
13. Speech intended to advise, incite or encourage
14. Stinky; smelly
15. Remained; tarried
16. Saved; used sparingly

A=2	B=3	C=15	D=14
E=13	F=16	G=4	H=1
I=8	J=5	K=9	L=12
M=11	N=10	O=6	P=7

The Grapes of Wrath Vocabulary Magic Squares 2

Match the definition with the vocabulary word. Put your answers in the magic squares below. When your answers are correct, all columns and rows will add to the same number.

A. ASSAILED
B. PINNACLES
C. SERENE
D. PUTRESCENCE
E. PALL
F. PRECIOUS
G. DENUNCIATION
H. DEMURE
I. IRRITABLY
J. FERAL
K. PRODIGAL
L. OBSCURED
M. CONSERVED
N. PROVOCATIVELY
O. CONTRITE
P. AGITATORS

1. Assaulted
2. In an exciting or stimulating way
3. Wild; savage
4. Gloomy atmosphere
5. Public condemnation
6. Hidden from view
7. People who stir up trouble
8. Calm, peaceful
9. Sorry
10. Rotten, decaying matter
11. Shy; modest; reserved
12. Extravagant
13. In a manner showing annoyance
14. Valuable
15. Tall, pointed formations
16. Saved; used sparingly

A=	B=	C=	D=
E=	F=	G=	H=
I=	J=	K=	L=
M=	N=	O=	P=

The Grapes of Wrath Vocabulary Magic Squares 2 Answer Key

Match the definition with the vocabulary word. Put your answers in the magic squares below. When your answers are correct, all columns and rows will add to the same number.

A. ASSAILED
B. PINNACLES
C. SERENE
D. PUTRESCENCE
E. PALL
F. PRECIOUS
G. DENUNCIATION
H. DEMURE
I. IRRITABLY
J. FERAL
K. PRODIGAL
L. OBSCURED
M. CONSERVED
N. PROVOCATIVELY
O. CONTRITE
P. AGITATORS

1. Assaulted
2. In an exciting or stimulating way
3. Wild; savage
4. Gloomy atmosphere
5. Public condemnation
6. Hidden from view
7. People who stir up trouble
8. Calm, peaceful
9. Sorry
10. Rotten, decaying matter
11. Shy; modest; reserved
12. Extravagant
13. In a manner showing annoyance
14. Valuable
15. Tall, pointed formations
16. Saved; used sparingly

A=1	B=15	C=8	D=10
E=4	F=14	G=5	H=11
I=13	J=3	K=12	L=6
M=16	N=2	O=9	P=7

The Grapes of Wrath Vocabulary Magic Squares 3

Match the definition with the vocabulary word. Put your answers in the magic squares below. When your answers are correct, all columns and rows will add to the same number.

A. LINGERED
B. FETID
C. SKULK
D. LUSTERLESS
E. PERPLEXITY
F. TIMBRE
G. HYPOCRITE
H. CONTRITE
I. ASSAILED
J. PARADOXES
K. FRET
L. PRECINCT
M. DENUNCIATION
N. APPREHENSION
O. INQUIRINGLY
P. NEBULOUS

1. Anxiousness
2. One who says he believes one way but in action shows he believes the opposite
3. District
4. Remained; tarried
5. Worry
6. Stinky; smelly
7. Public condemnation
8. Sorry
9. Confusion; puzzlement
10. Lacking definite form
11. Lurk; lie in hiding
12. Seemingly contradictory aspects
13. Dull
14. Assaulted
15. Distinguishing quality of a sound
16. Questioningly

A=	B=	C=	D=
E=	F=	G=	H=
I=	J=	K=	L=
M=	N=	O=	P=

The Grapes of Wrath Vocabulary Magic Squares 3 Answer Key

Match the definition with the vocabulary word. Put your answers in the magic squares below. When your answers are correct, all columns and rows will add to the same number.

A. LINGERED
B. FETID
C. SKULK
D. LUSTERLESS
E. PERPLEXITY
F. TIMBRE
G. HYPOCRITE
H. CONTRITE
I. ASSAILED
J. PARADOXES
K. FRET
L. PRECINCT
M. DENUNCIATION
N. APPREHENSION
O. INQUIRINGLY
P. NEBULOUS

1. Anxiousness
2. One who says he believes one way but in action shows he believes the opposite
3. District
4. Remained; tarried
5. Worry
6. Stinky; smelly
7. Public condemnation
8. Sorry
9. Confusion; puzzlement
10. Lacking definite form
11. Lurk; lie in hiding
12. Seemingly contradictory aspects
13. Dull
14. Assaulted
15. Distinguishing quality of a sound
16. Questioningly

A=4	B=6	C=11	D=13
E=9	F=15	G=2	H=8
I=14	J=12	K=5	L=3
M=7	N=1	O=16	P=10

The Grapes of Wrath Vocabulary Magic Squares 4

Match the definition with the vocabulary word. Put your answers in the magic squares below. When your answers are correct, all columns and rows will add to the same number.

A. DECLIVITY
B. RECEDED
C. ENGAGINGLY
D. IRRITABLY
E. PARADOXES
F. FERAL
G. FETID
H. CONTRITE
I. TIMBRE
J. PINNACLES
K. LINGERED
L. PUTRESCENCE
M. DISCONSOLATE
N. ALOOF
O. PRECIOUS
P. VITALITY

1. Sorry
2. Dejected; gloomy
3. Withdrew
4. Remained; tarried
5. Tall, pointed formations
6. Charmingly; attractively
7. Energy; liveliness
8. Seemingly contradictory aspects
9. Valuable
10. Wild; savage
11. Distinguishing quality of a sound
12. In a manner showing annoyance
13. Slope; hill
14. Rotten, decaying matter
15. Stinky; smelly
16. Reserved; distant

A=	B=	C=	D=
E=	F=	G=	H=
I=	J=	K=	L=
M=	N=	O=	P=

The Grapes of Wrath Vocabulary Magic Squares 4 Answer Key

Match the definition with the vocabulary word. Put your answers in the magic squares below. When your answers are correct, all columns and rows will add to the same number.

A. DECLIVITY
B. RECEDED
C. ENGAGINGLY
D. IRRITABLY
E. PARADOXES
F. FERAL
G. FETID
H. CONTRITE
I. TIMBRE
J. PINNACLES
K. LINGERED
L. PUTRESCENCE
M. DISCONSOLATE
N. ALOOF
O. PRECIOUS
P. VITALITY

1. Sorry
2. Dejected; gloomy
3. Withdrew
4. Remained; tarried
5. Tall, pointed formations
6. Charmingly; attractively
7. Energy; liveliness
8. Seemingly contradictory aspects
9. Valuable
10. Wild; savage
11. Distinguishing quality of a sound
12. In a manner showing annoyance
13. Slope; hill
14. Rotten, decaying matter
15. Stinky; smelly
16. Reserved; distant

A=13	B=3	C=6	D=12
E=8	F=10	G=15	H=1
I=11	J=5	K=4	L=14
M=2	N=16	O=9	P=7

The Grapes of Wrath Vocabulary Word Search 1

```
S A L D E R E T N U A S P G B K T Q R W
G N Y P Q M F L D E N E R E S Q I Y Z T
R L G M E S T E E P J B E B T R M D Q Z
E A X R F T V A R H A F C T E X B E F Q
C G G D S R M I U A L N I F W S R R W Q
E E P R E C I N C T L C O N Q U E S T C
D N G S X C K Q S J C O U R M T T E K Y
E M N P O X L U B P L C S E A N G C C P
D O O D D W S I O A K K D F E M Y X I H
C Y S K A L Y R V S R J W M E L I D N M
V L T W R I L I V I X E R Y P T E C S Z
I I R P A N E N F N T E A L T F I Z I X
T K A A P G V G W O T Y C S L X P D G Q
A L C G F E I L S U R C C U S V H K N B
L U I I A R T Y O K V L G O L U A J I J
I S S T T E A C L W U N O I N V R G A Q
T H M A U D C N A I E L N R P T E E U L
Y H F T O A O F C Z T K K U N V R R D E
G Z Y O U S V P I E W H K X M J F I T X
B Z L R S M O V N N D Y E U J M W S T M
X L P S L V R G Y E D D E L I A S S A E
N D Z K Y G P B C D N S X V Y H Q F R H
```

Accessories (13)
Accomplishment; having overcome something (8)
As an indulgence; not necessarily out of necessity (11)
Assaulted (8)
Being shunned or ignored by the group (9)
Calm, peaceful (6)
Came out (7)
Distinguishing quality of a sound (6)
District (8)
Drainage ditch (7)
Emblem (8)
Energy; liveliness (8)
Gloomily; in a withdrawn manner (7)
Gloomy atmosphere (4)
Gracefully (7)
Hidden from view (8)
In an exciting or stimulating way (13)
Initial cell structure from which a part or organ develops; foundation (6)
Lurk; lie in hiding (5)
Make an earnest request (7)
Not clearly expressive (5)
People who stir up trouble (9)
Questioningly (11)
Remained; tarried (8)
Reserved; distant (5)
Restored confidence (9)
Sad because of being abandoned (7)
Saved; used sparingly (9)
Scornful of the motives, virtue or integrity of others (7)
Seemingly contradictory aspects (9)
Shy; modest; reserved (6)
Slope; hill (9)
Smugly (9)
Sorry (8)
Stinky; smelly (5)
Strolled (9)
Swallowed up; surrounded; enclosed (8)
Tight; tense (4)
Valuable (8)
Wild; savage (5)
With a wide view (9)
Withdrew (7)
Withered; wrinkled (7)
Worry (4)

The Grapes of Wrath Vocabulary Word Search 1 Answer Key

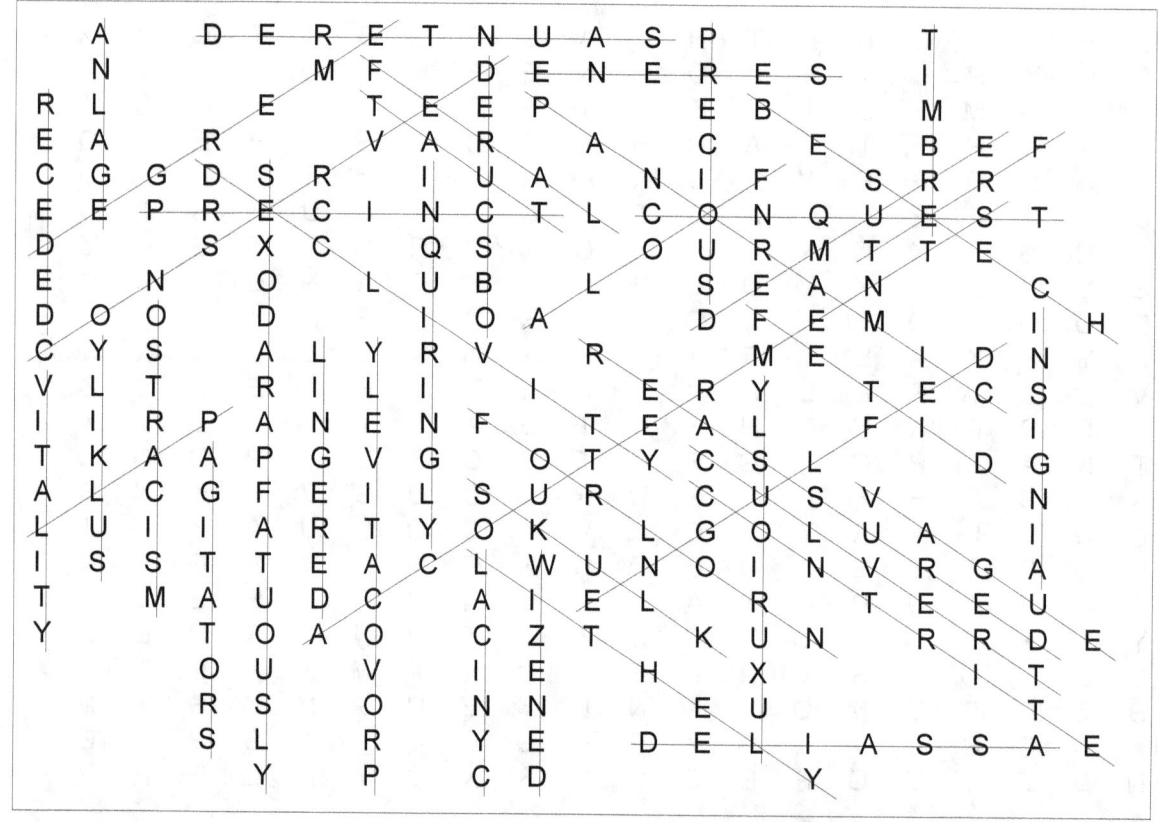

Accessories (13)
Accomplishment; having overcome something (8)
As an indulgence;not necessarily out of necessity (11)
Assaulted (8)
Being shunned or ignored by the group (9)
Calm, peaceful (6)
Came out (7)
Distinguishing quality of a sound (6)
District (8)
Drainage ditch (7)
Emblem (8)
Energy; liveliness (8)
Gloomily; in a withdrawn manner (7)
Gloomy atmosphere (4)
Gracefully (7)
Hidden from view (8)
In an exciting or stimulating way (13)
Initial cell structure from which a part or organ develops; foundation (6)
Lurk; lie in hiding (5)
Make an earnest request (7)
Not clearly expressive (5)

People who stir up trouble (9)
Questioningly (11)
Remained; tarried (8)
Reserved; distant (5)
Restored confidence (9)
Sad because of being abandoned (7)
Saved; used sparingly (9)
Scornful of the motives, virtue or integrity of others (7)
Seemingly contradictory aspects (9)
Shy; modest; reserved (6)
Slope; hill (9)
Smugly (9)
Sorry (8)
Stinky; smelly (5)
Strolled (9)
Swallowed up; surrounded; enclosed (8)
Tight; tense (4)
Valuable (8)
Wild; savage (5)
With a wide view (9)
Withdrew (7)
Withered; wrinkled (7)
Worry (4)

The Grapes of Wrath Vocabulary Word Search 2

```
I V I T A L I T Y L I K L U S D D S Z K
P N M X A G I T A T O R S J E E U I Z
V C S H K F N G C H Q D R L R O O M Z
P I T I W Q I H Y F E W I U R C S I P S
E M V Z G D G W N F V A C E Y U T C E K
R A K A O N B S I V S S K H L L R E R S
P R X R C T I A C S B N G T S V A R T M
L O P N D I N A A O A F P D U E C P U V
E N B D E T O D L T V A F S O R I L R D
X A V G L B E U N Q B T F O I T S I B M
I P A Y V D U A S J G U X N R S M N A P
T P G Y E X C L C N B O T E E L D G B D
Y D U C D N G W O P E U A I P E O E L K
F G E I A G G K L U K S N W M L A R E F
N R T C N P D A W K S L S U I B P E N L
N E D C L H R T G U G Y R E F Z R D B S
F O O L A I F E R I L E V C R B E E E N
G K G S G N V E C E N P N Q E E V N S T
P T Z W E P D I H I T G Z C T M N L E K
E M E R G E D T T U N N L F D Y L E E D
Q G N I C N I M A Y B C X Y Y A B J C D
Z M O D U L A T E D R Q T Z P Q R R H V
```

Assaulted (8)
Authoritatively (11)
Being shunned or ignored by the group (9)
Calm, peaceful (6)
Came out (7)
Can't be upset or annoyed (13)
Charmingly; attractively (10)
Confusion; puzzlement (10)
Distinguishing quality of a sound (6)
District (8)
Drainage ditch (7)
Emblem (8)
Energy; liveliness (8)
Extravagant (8)
Gloomily; in a withdrawn manner (7)
Gloomy atmosphere (4)
Gracefully (7)
Hidden from view (8)
Ill-tempered; difficult to handle (12)
In a manner rejecting authority (9)
Initial cell structure from which a part or organ develops; foundation (6)
Lacking definite form (8)
Liveliness; animation (13)
Lurk; lie in hiding (5)
Make an earnest request (7)
Not clearly expressive (5)
People who stir up trouble (9)
Remained; tarried (8)
Reserved; distant (5)
Restored confidence (9)
Sad because of being abandoned (7)
Scornful of the motives, virtue or integrity of others (7)
Shy; modest; reserved (6)
Slope; hill (9)
Smugly (9)
Stinky; smelly (5)
Tight; tense (4)
Valuable (8)
Walking with short steps (7)
Wild; savage (5)
With a varying tone (9)
With a wide view (9)
Withdrew (7)
Withered; wrinkled (7)
Worry (4)

The Grapes of Wrath Vocabulary Word Search 2 Answer Key

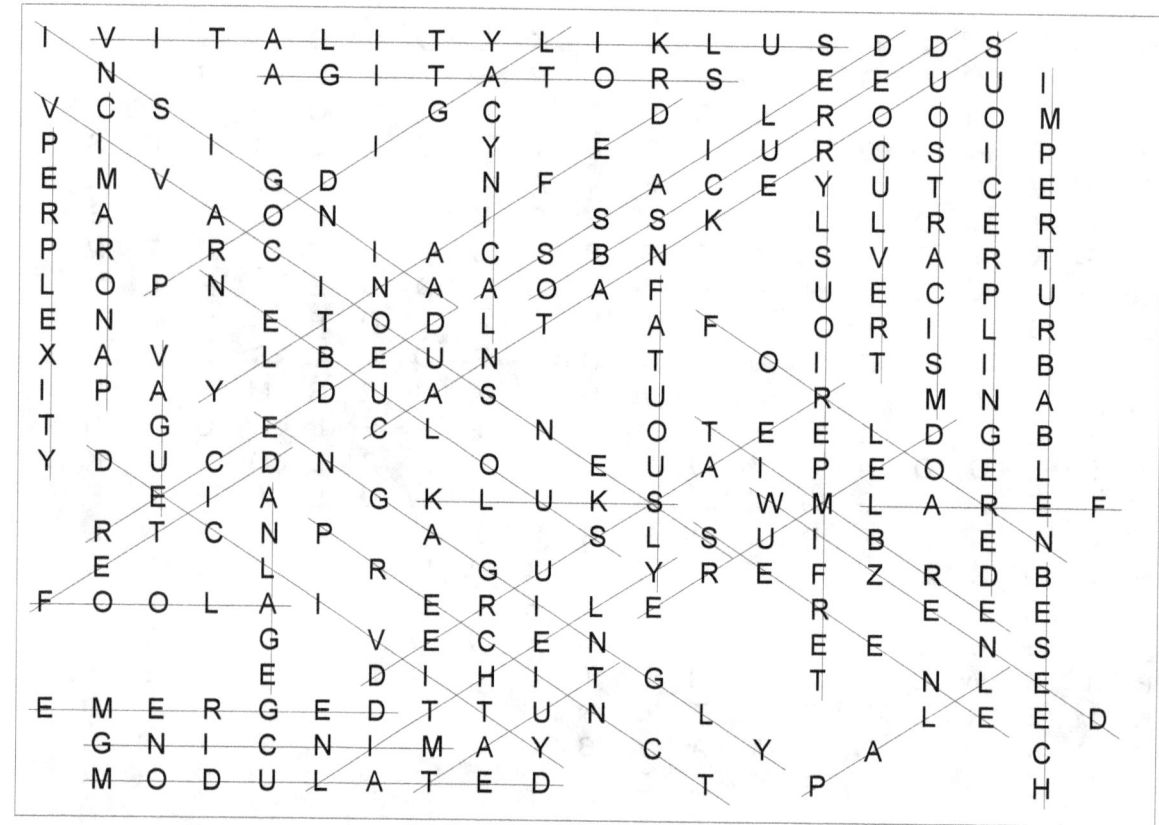

Assaulted (8)
Authoritatively (11)
Being shunned or ignored by the group (9)
Calm, peaceful (6)
Came out (7)
Can't be upset or annoyed (13)
Charmingly; attractively (10)
Confusion; puzzlement (10)
Distinguishing quality of a sound (6)
District (8)
Drainage ditch (7)
Emblem (8)
Energy; liveliness (8)
Extravagant (8)
Gloomily; in a withdrawn manner (7)
Gloomy atmosphere (4)
Gracefully (7)
Hidden from view (8)
Ill-tempered; difficult to handle (12)
In a manner rejecting authority (9)
Initial cell structure from which a part or organ develops; foundation (6)
Lacking definite form (8)
Liveliness; animation (13)

Lurk; lie in hiding (5)
Make an earnest request (7)
Not clearly expressive (5)
People who stir up trouble (9)
Remained; tarried (8)
Reserved; distant (5)
Restored confidence (9)
Sad because of being abandoned (7)
Scornful of the motives, virtue or integrity of others (7)
Shy; modest; reserved (6)
Slope; hill (9)
Smugly (9)
Stinky; smelly (5)
Tight; tense (4)
Valuable (8)
Walking with short steps (7)
Wild; savage (5)
With a varying tone (9)
With a wide view (9)
Withdrew (7)
Withered; wrinkled (7)
Worry (4)

The Grapes of Wrath Vocabulary Word Search 3

F	A	T	U	O	U	S	L	Y	C	U	L	V	E	R	T	S	A	D	W
F	L	N	B	B	Y	U	S	T	N	R	B	G	B	I	S	I	E	H	S
P	O	D	D	G	C	L	G	I	E	R	P	Y	M	E	N	R	M	U	N
K	O	T	E	F	G	K	G	L	T	B	F	B	L	G	E	H	O	R	N
Y	F	W	R	L	M	I	T	A	A	F	R	R	I	G	Y	L	O	C	V
L	N	X	U	Y	T	L	Q	T	L	E	E	S	N	R	U	L	S	P	C
T	G	A	S	H	G	Y	N	I	O	T	N	I	D	B	R	B	A	A	T
N	K	N	S	S	V	P	F	V	S	I	L	O	E	O	P	X	U	N	C
E	V	M	A	S	W	R	R	U	N	S	B	N	F	D	D	V	N	O	X
L	G	L	E	V	A	G	L	E	O	S	V	G	L	W	E	J	T	R	J
U	X	A	R	T	N	I	Y	M	C	F	X	A	U	T	M	T	E	A	S
C	G	C	F	I	Y	F	L	U	S	I	J	G	G	F	U	X	R	M	R
U	O	I	C	V	P	R	R	E	I	N	N	B	N	U	R	L	E	I	M
R	L	N	D	I	T	E	F	W	D	R	E	C	E	D	E	D	D	C	N
T	I	Y	C	L	D	T	R	E	I	S	T	N	T	C	N	E	E	O	V
M	T	C	A	E	B	P	C	P	E	Z	E	A	H	B	G	R	F	N	D
J	H	R	P	J	S	L	R	E	L	R	E	E	U	R	A	A	I	S	R
J	E	A	C	R	I	S	C	O	E	E	R	N	E	T	G	N	A	E	J
F	L	H	B	V	E	H	I	S	D	O	X	M	E	I	I	S	N	R	R
L	Y	X	I	S	V	C	E	O	U	I	E	I	T	D	N	N	T	V	H
J	S	T	X	K	X	G	I	S	N	H	G	A	T	G	G	E	L	E	Y
H	Y	F	W	U	A	J	N	O	C	K	T	A	R	Y	L	G	Y	D	R
M	O	D	U	L	A	T	E	D	U	O	N	W	L	J	Y	L	Z	X	L
G	K	L	N	K	H	M	D	L	R	S	O	S	T	R	A	C	I	S	M
D	P	A	V	W	B	Y	L	S	U	O	I	R	U	X	U	L	Y	Y	G

AGITATORS	EMERGED	LUSTERLESS	REASSURED
ALOOF	ENGAGINGLY	LUXURIOUSLY	RECEDED
ANLAGE	ENGULFED	MINCING	SAUNTERED
ASSAILED	ENSNARED	MODULATED	SERENE
BESEECH	FATUOUSLY	NEBULOUS	SKULK
CONCESSION	FERAL	OBSCURED	SULKILY
CONSERVED	FETID	OSTRACISM	TAUT
CULVERT	FORLORN	PALL	TIMBRE
CYNICAL	FRET	PANORAMIC	TRUCULENTLY
DECLIVITY	INSIGNIA	PERPLEXITY	VAGUE
DEFIANTLY	LECHEROUS	PRECINCT	VITALITY
DEMURE	LINGERED	PRECIOUS	WIZENED
DISCONSOLATE	LITHELY	PRODIGAL	

The Grapes of Wrath Vocabulary Word Search 3 Answer Key

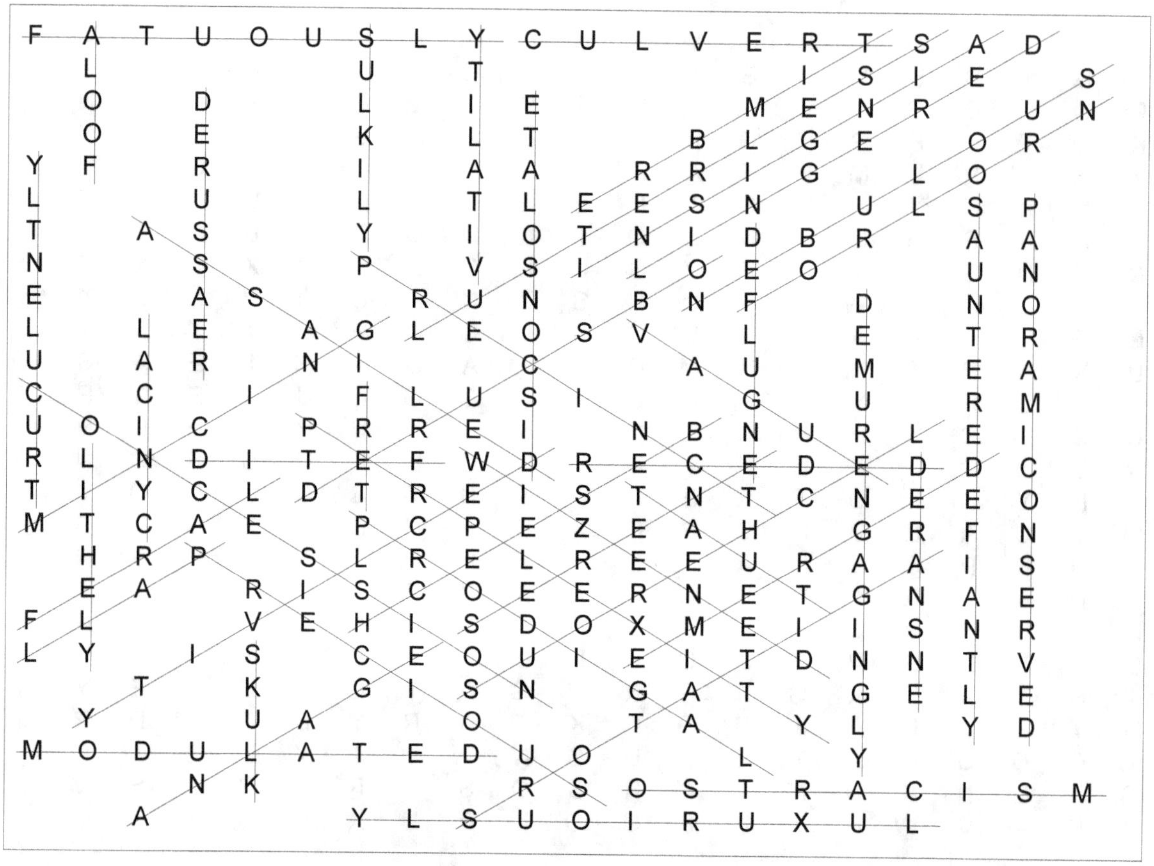

AGITATORS	EMERGED	LUSTERLESS	REASSURED
ALOOF	ENGAGINGLY	LUXURIOUSLY	RECEDED
ANLAGE	ENGULFED	MINCING	SAUNTERED
ASSAILED	ENSNARED	MODULATED	SERENE
BESEECH	FATUOUSLY	NEBULOUS	SKULK
CONCESSION	FERAL	OBSCURED	SULKILY
CONSERVED	FETID	OSTRACISM	TAUT
CULVERT	FORLORN	PALL	TIMBRE
CYNICAL	FRET	PANORAMIC	TRUCULENTLY
DECLIVITY	INSIGNIA	PERPLEXITY	VAGUE
DEFIANTLY	LECHEROUS	PRECINCT	VITALITY
DEMURE	LINGERED	PRECIOUS	WIZENED
DISCONSOLATE	LITHELY	PRODIGAL	

The Grapes of Wrath Vocabulary Word Search 4

```
L I T H E L Y C E N G U L F E D P A L L
U D P S N S M I Y C F A A I J Z U L A L
X I I E S Y M M V N G D C E N G T O R Z
U S R S Y G H A D I D S I N M G R O E C
R C C E N M G R D E E S N G O Q E F F V
I O S N A U E O F L F M Y A D S S R H Z
O N E E R A R N C L S I C G U U C B E T
U S D Y E P P A R V N A I L L E T D
S O N G Z T N P O C L C Y N A K N S I H
L L O V E N D T R V I I H G T I C R C
Y A N R I S A E J E S N W L E L E C L
T T F P A T P G N U H G G Y D Y Y C O R
I E Y C I V A A O U K E I L G F J H P M
V P C G U F E L D P N Y N N Y S E N Y Q
I E A O Q L U N I E L C S S S T O T H G
L R P K N B V A O T M H I W I I A S I T
C P L A E Q G E N U Y U D A T O G U C D
E L F N R P U E R L S E R A T E N N T X
D E Z O P A L E S T V K G E R I I Z I T
Z X Q L R U D U S R R I U B C C O H Z A
Y I B F C L O O E T L X M L E E H N F K
C T H U Q U O S X B M I P R K Z D G R F
K Y R H T L N R O E T D P D E G R E M F
W T R A W O G G N A S S A I L E D T D V
B W F R C O N C E S S I O N Q G F N Q N
```

AGITATORS	DENUNCIATION	LITHELY	PRODIGAL
ALOOF	DISCONSOLATE	LUXURIOUSLY	PUTRESCENCE
ANLAGE	EMERGED	MENACINGLY	RAVENOUS
APPREHENSION	ENGAGINGLY	MINCING	RECEDED
ASSAILED	ENGULFED	MODULATED	SERENE
BESEECH	ENSNARED	NEBULOUS	SKULK
CONCESSION	FATUOUSLY	NONDESCRIPT	SULKILY
CONQUEST	FERAL	OBLIGATION	TAUT
CONSERVED	FETID	PALL	TIMBRE
CULVERT	FORLORN	PANORAMIC	TRUCULENTLY
CYNICAL	FRET	PARADOXES	VAGUE
DECLIVITY	HYPOCRITE	PERPLEXITY	VITALITY
DEFIANTLY	INSIGNIA	PINNACLES	
DEMURE	LINGERED	PRECINCT	

The Grapes of Wrath Vocabulary Word Search 4 Answer Key

AGITATORS	DENUNCIATION	LITHELY	PRODIGAL
ALOOF	DISCONSOLATE	LUXURIOUSLY	PUTRESCENCE
ANLAGE	EMERGED	MENACINGLY	RAVENOUS
APPREHENSION	ENGAGINGLY	MINCING	RECEDED
ASSAILED	ENGULFED	MODULATED	SERENE
BESEECH	ENSNARED	NEBULOUS	SKULK
CONCESSION	FATUOUSLY	NONDESCRIPT	SULKILY
CONQUEST	FERAL	OBLIGATION	TAUT
CONSERVED	FETID	PALL	TIMBRE
CULVERT	FORLORN	PANORAMIC	TRUCULENTLY
CYNICAL	FRET	PARADOXES	VAGUE
DECLIVITY	HYPOCRITE	PERPLEXITY	VITALITY
DEFIANTLY	INSIGNIA	PINNACLES	
DEMURE	LINGERED	PRECINCT	

The Grapes of Wrath Vocabulary Crossword 1

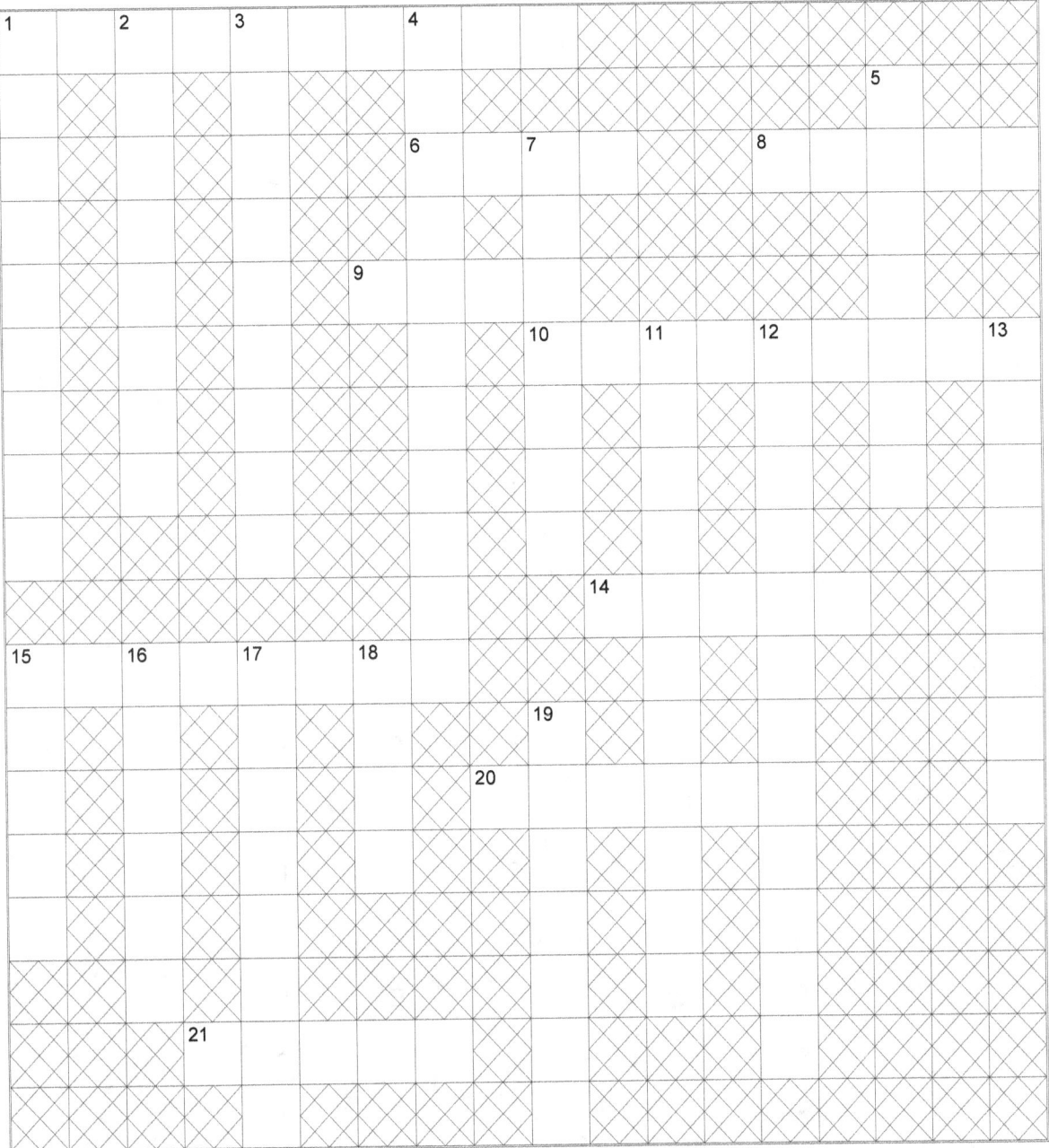

Across
1. Confusion; puzzlement
6. Gloomy atmosphere
8. Lurk; lie in hiding
9. Worry
10. One who says he believes one way but in action shows he believes the opposite
14. Wild; savage
15. Energy; liveliness
20. Calm, peaceful
21. Stinky; smelly

Down
1. Tall, pointed formations
2. Extremely hungry
3. Tending towards excessive promiscuous behavior
4. Authoritatively
5. Gloomily; in a withdrawn manner
7. Gracefully
11. Rotten, decaying matter
12. Ill-tempered; difficult to handle
13. Swallowed up; surrounded; enclosed
15. Not clearly expressive
16. Distinguishing quality of a sound
17. Remained; tarried
18. Tight; tense
19. Make an earnest request

The Grapes of Wrath Vocabulary Crossword 1 Answer Key

Across
1. Confusion; puzzlement
6. Gloomy atmosphere
8. Lurk; lie in hiding
9. Worry
10. One who says he believes one way but in action shows he believes the opposite
14. Wild; savage
15. Energy; liveliness
20. Calm, peaceful
21. Stinky; smelly

Down
1. Tall, pointed formations
2. Extremely hungry
3. Tending towards excessive promiscuous behavior
4. Authoritatively
5. Gloomily; in a withdrawn manner
7. Gracefully
11. Rotten, decaying matter
12. Ill-tempered; difficult to handle
13. Swallowed up; surrounded; enclosed
15. Not clearly expressive
16. Distinguishing quality of a sound
17. Remained; tarried
18. Tight; tense
19. Make an earnest request

The Grapes of Wrath Vocabulary Crossword 2

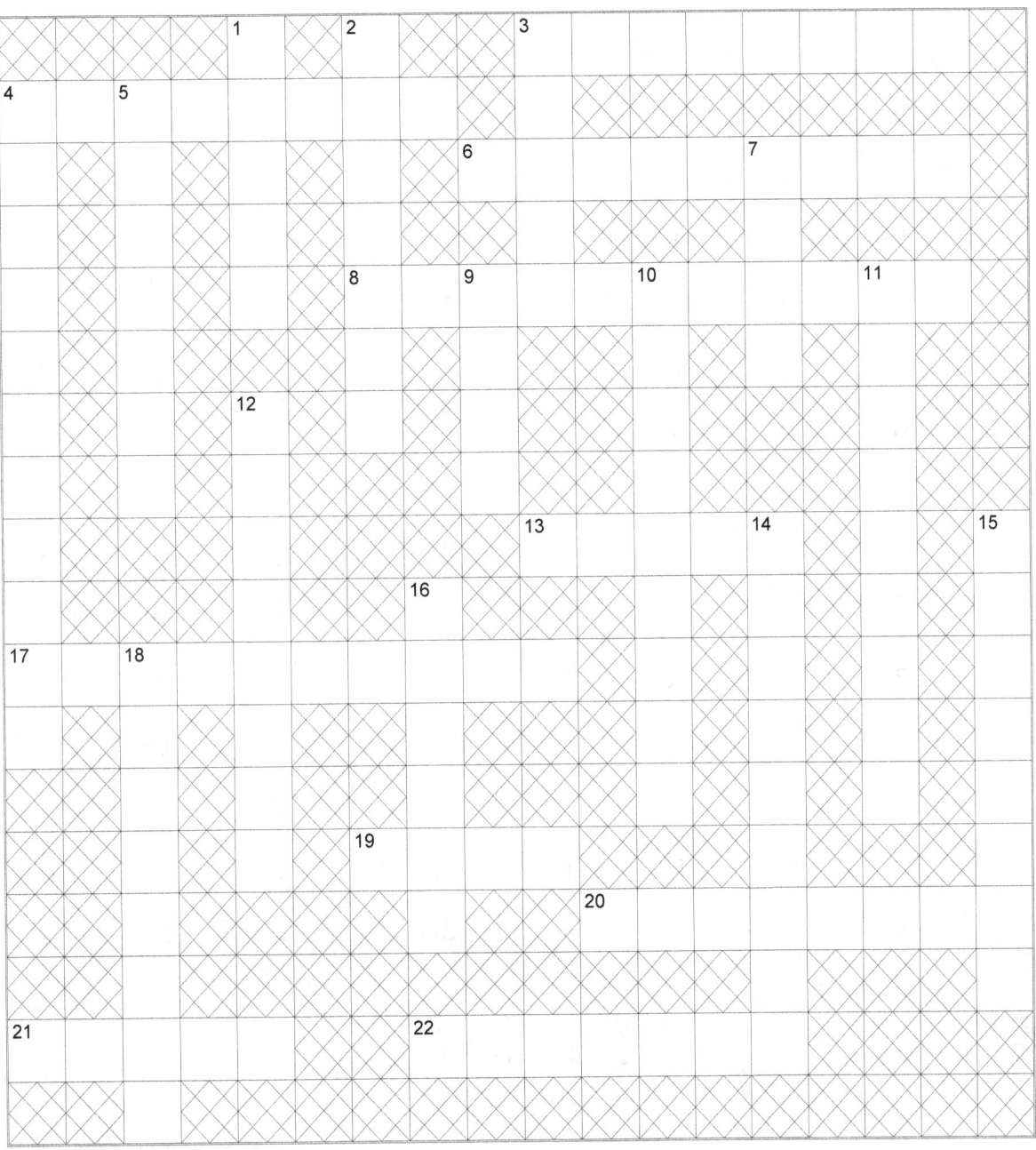

Across
3. Energy; liveliness
4. Lacking definite form
6. People who stir up trouble
8. Authoritatively
13. Stinky; smelly
17. Confusion; puzzlement
19. Worry
20. Sorry
21. Lurk; lie in hiding
22. Gracefully

Down
1. Reserved; distant
2. Gloomily; in a withdrawn manner
3. Not clearly expressive
4. Having no individual, distinguishing characteristics
5. Make an earnest request
7. Tight; tense
9. Gloomy atmosphere
10. In a manner showing annoyance
11. Tending towards excessive promiscuous behavior
12. Swallowed up; surrounded; enclosed
14. In a manner rejecting authority
15. Assaulted
16. Distinguishing quality of a sound
18. Extremely hungry

The Grapes of Wrath Vocabulary Crossword 2 Answer Key

Across
3. Energy; liveliness
4. Lacking definite form
6. People who stir up trouble
8. Authoritatively
13. Stinky; smelly
17. Confusion; puzzlement
19. Worry
20. Sorry
21. Lurk; lie in hiding
22. Gracefully

Down
1. Reserved; distant
2. Gloomily; in a withdrawn manner
3. Not clearly expressive
4. Having no individual, distinguishing characteristics
5. Make an earnest request
7. Tight; tense
9. Gloomy atmosphere
10. In a manner showing annoyance
11. Tending towards excessive promiscuous behavior
12. Swallowed up; surrounded; enclosed
14. In a manner rejecting authority
15. Assaulted
16. Distinguishing quality of a sound
18. Extremely hungry

The Grapes of Wrath Vocabulary Crossword 3

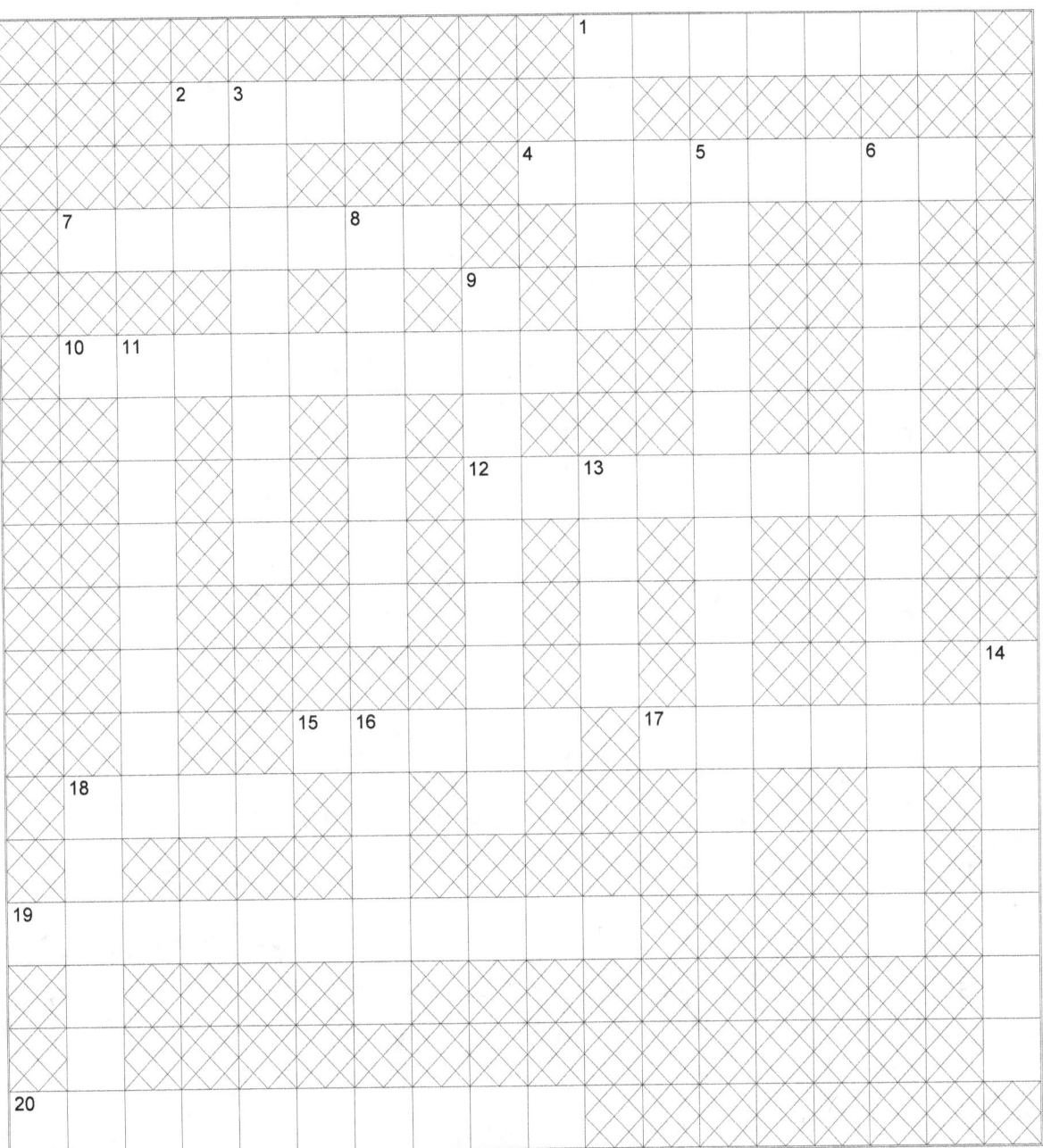

Across
1. Sad because of being abandoned
2. Worry
4. Extravagant
7. Drainage ditch
10. Tall, pointed formations
12. One who says he believes one way but in action shows he believes the opposite
15. Not clearly expressive
17. Gracefully
18. Tight; tense
19. Authoritatively
20. Confusion; puzzlement

Down
1. Wild; savage
3. Extremely hungry
5. Public condemnation
6. Accessories
8. Withdrew
9. Tending towards excessive promiscuous behavior
11. Emblem
13. Gloomy atmosphere
14. Scornful of the motives, virtue or integrity of others
16. Reserved; distant
18. Distinguishing quality of a sound

The Grapes of Wrath Vocabulary Crossword 3 Answer Key

Across
1. Sad because of being abandoned
2. Worry
4. Extravagant
7. Drainage ditch
10. Tall, pointed formations
12. One who says he believes one way but in action shows he believes the opposite
15. Not clearly expressive
17. Gracefully
18. Tight; tense
19. Authoritatively
20. Confusion; puzzlement

Down
1. Wild; savage
3. Extremely hungry
5. Public condemnation
6. Accessories
8. Withdrew
9. Tending towards excessive promiscuous behavior
11. Emblem
13. Gloomy atmosphere
14. Scornful of the motives, virtue or integrity of others
16. Reserved; distant
18. Distinguishing quality of a sound

The Grapes of Wrath Vocabulary Crossword 4

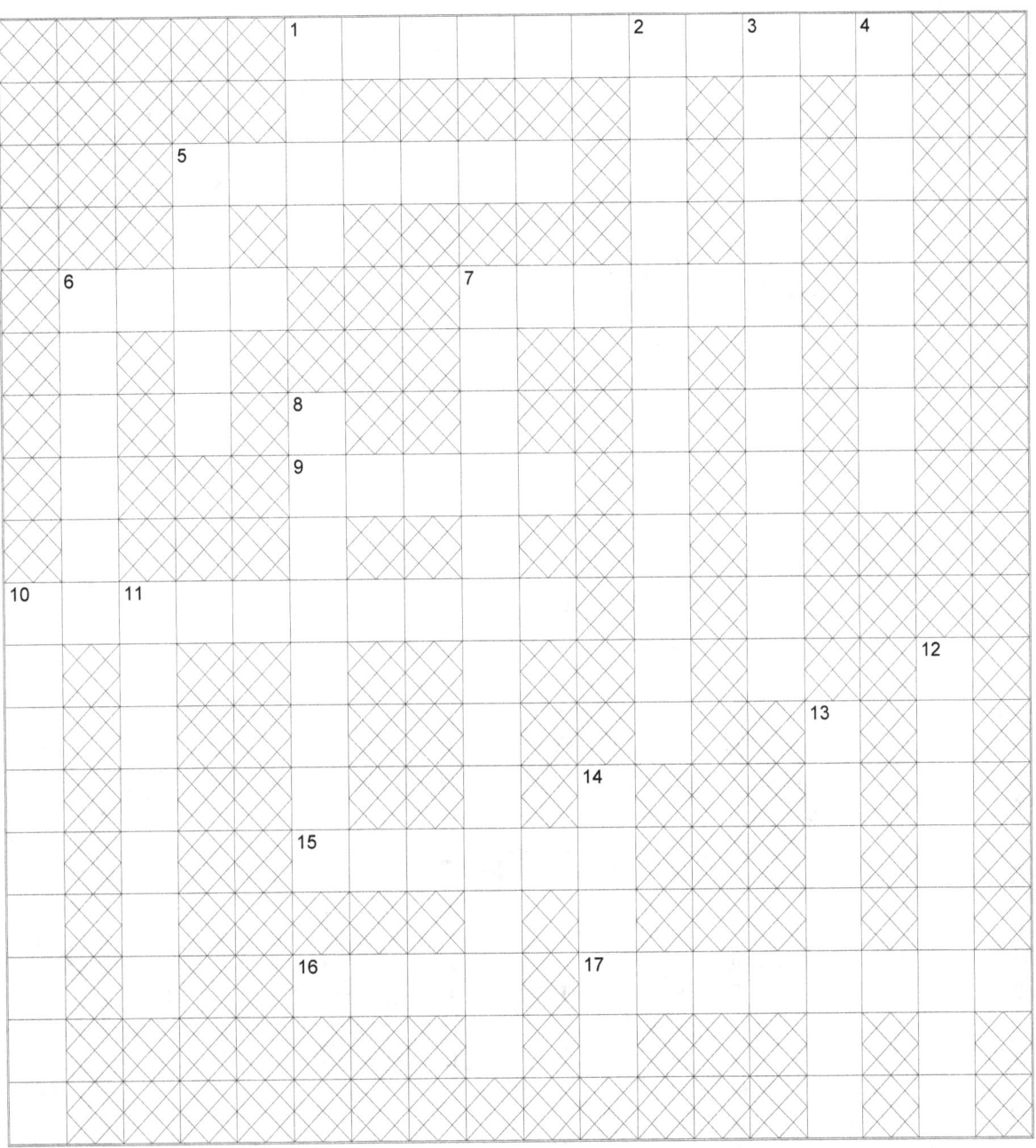

Across
1. Rotten, decaying matter
5. Gloomily; in a withdrawn manner
6. Tight; tense
7. Initial cell structure from which a part or organ develops; foundation
9. Reserved; distant
10. Confusion; puzzlement
15. Calm, peaceful
16. Worry
17. Assaulted

Down
1. Gloomy atmosphere
2. Ill-tempered; difficult to handle
3. Having no individual, distinguishing characteristics
4. Swallowed up; surrounded; enclosed
5. Lurk; lie in hiding
6. Distinguishing quality of a sound
7. Accessories
8. Extremely hungry
10. Tall, pointed formations
11. Withdrew
12. Accomplishment; having overcome something
13. Walking with short steps
14. Wild; savage

The Grapes of Wrath Vocabulary Crossword 4 Answer Key

Across
1. Rotten, decaying matter
5. Gloomily; in a withdrawn manner
6. Tight; tense
7. Initial cell structure from which a part or organ develops; foundation
9. Reserved; distant
10. Confusion; puzzlement
15. Calm, peaceful
16. Worry
17. Assaulted

Down
1. Gloomy atmosphere
2. Ill-tempered; difficult to handle
3. Having no individual, distinguishing characteristics
4. Swallowed up; surrounded; enclosed
5. Lurk; lie in hiding
6. Distinguishing quality of a sound
7. Accessories
8. Extremely hungry
10. Tall, pointed formations
11. Withdrew
12. Accomplishment; having overcome something
13. Walking with short steps
14. Wild; savage

The Grapes of Wrath Vocabulary Juggle Letters 1

1. TFIDE = 1. _____
   Stinky; smelly

2. RDUBCSEO = 2. _____
   Hidden from view

3. UIUOLYSRUXL = 3. _____
   As an indulgence; not necessarily out of necessity

4. LALP = 4. _____
   Gloomy atmosphere

5. ESHEORCLU = 5. _____
   Tending towards excessive promiscuous behavior

6. CPNIOAMRA = 6. _____
   With a wide view

7. GNOIIAOTLB = 7. _____
   Duty; contract; promise

8. SREAUREDS = 8. _____
   Restored confidence

9. SUQCTOEN = 9. _____
   Accomplishment; having overcome something

10. UEGVA = 10. _____
    Not clearly expressive

11. EDIZEWN = 11. _____
    Withered; wrinkled

12. USOARVNE = 12. _____
    Extremely hungry

13. ETLBRIEMAPBUR = 13. _____
    Can't be upset or annoyed

14. YLDEVTICI = 14. _____
    Slope; hill

15. IAOTGRATS = 15. _____
    People who stir up trouble

The Grapes of Wrath Vocabulary Juggle Letters 1 Answer Key

1. TFIDE = 1. FETID
   Stinky; smelly

2. RDUBCSEO = 2. OBSCURED
   Hidden from view

3. UIUOLYSRUXL = 3. LUXURIOUSLY
   As an indulgence; not necessarily out of necessity

4. LALP = 4. PALL
   Gloomy atmosphere

5. ESHEORCLU = 5. LECHEROUS
   Tending towards excessive promiscuous behavior

6. CPNIOAMRA = 6. PANORAMIC
   With a wide view

7. GNOIIAOTLB = 7. OBLIGATION
   Duty; contract; promise

8. SREAUREDS = 8. REASSURED
   Restored confidence

9. SUQCTOEN = 9. CONQUEST
   Accomplishment; having overcome something

10. UEGVA = 10. VAGUE
    Not clearly expressive

11. EDIZEWN = 11. WIZENED
    Withered; wrinkled

12. USOARVNE = 12. RAVENOUS
    Extremely hungry

13. ETLBRIEMAPBUR = 13. IMPERTURBABLE
    Can't be upset or annoyed

14. YLDEVTICI = 14. DECLIVITY
    Slope; hill

15. IAOTGRATS = 15. AGITATORS
    People who stir up trouble

Copyrighted

The Grapes of Wrath Vocabulary Juggle Letters 2

1. TCTAONRCUMESE = 1. _____
   Accessories

2. OUPCRISE = 2. _____
   Valuable

3. DDETOUMLA = 3. _____
   With a varying tone

4. SQUNTEOC = 4. _____
   Accomplishment; having overcome something

5. IBMTER = 5. _____
   Distinguishing quality of a sound

6. EREDEGM = 6. _____
   Came out

7. OAENNNIIDCUT = 7. _____
   Public condemnation

8. SSLUTLESER = 8. _____
   Dull

9. UCRENEPSTCE = 9. _____
   Rotten, decaying matter

10. NRLFORO = 10. _____
    Sad because of being abandoned

11. ETRLUCV = 11. _____
    Drainage ditch

12. PALL = 12. _____
    Gloomy atmosphere

13. DEMURE = 13. _____
    Shy; modest; reserved

14. OEVCRNESD = 14. _____
    Saved; used sparingly

15. ERNESE = 15. _____
    Calm, peaceful

The Grapes of Wrath Vocabulary Juggle Letters 2 Answer Key

1. TCTAONRCUMESE = 1. ACCOUTERMENTS
   Accessories

2. OUPCRISE = 2. PRECIOUS
   Valuable

3. DDETOUMLA = 3. MODULATED
   With a varying tone

4. SQUNTEOC = 4. CONQUEST
   Accomplishment; having overcome something

5. IBMTER = 5. TIMBRE
   Distinguishing quality of a sound

6. EREDEGM = 6. EMERGED
   Came out

7. OAENNNIIDCUT = 7. DENUNCIATION
   Public condemnation

8. SSLUTLESER = 8. LUSTERLESS
   Dull

9. UCRENEPSTCE = 9. PUTRESCENCE
   Rotten, decaying matter

10. NRLFORO = 10. FORLORN
    Sad because of being abandoned

11. ETRLUCV = 11. CULVERT
    Drainage ditch

12. PALL = 12. PALL
    Gloomy atmosphere

13. DEMURE = 13. DEMURE
    Shy; modest; reserved

14. OEVCRNESD = 14. CONSERVED
    Saved; used sparingly

15. ERNESE = 15. SERENE
    Calm, peaceful

The Grapes of Wrath Vocabulary Juggle Letters 3

1. NNIIIGSA = 1. _____
   Emblem

2. OARSAIGTT = 2. _____
   People who stir up trouble

3. ECITLDYIV = 3. _____
   Slope; hill

4. ECLLRTUYNUT = 4. _____
   Fiercely

5. UACMTEOESCRNT = 5. _____
   Accessories

6. FELNADIYT = 6. _____
   In a manner rejecting authority

7. CIROOVEPTLVYA = 7. _____
   In an exciting or stimulating way

8. NICGNMI = 8. _____
   Walking with short steps

9. OORRRTEPIP = 9. _____
   Owner

10. ATDRNESEU =10. _____
    Strolled

11. NIORTTEC =11. _____
    Sorry

12. DRSCNIOTNPE =12. _____
    Having no individual, distinguishing characteristics

13. NAOMAIRCP =13. _____
    With a wide view

14. EDMEGER =14. _____
    Came out

15. CMGNLYAIEN =15. _____
    Threateningly

The Grapes of Wrath Vocabulary Juggle Letters 3 Answer Key

1. NNIIIGSA = 1. INSIGNIA
   Emblem

2. OARSAIGTT = 2. AGITATORS
   People who stir up trouble

3. ECITLDYIV = 3. DECLIVITY
   Slope; hill

4. ECLLRTUYNUT = 4. TRUCULENTLY
   Fiercely

5. UACMTEOESCRNT = 5. ACCOUTERMENTS
   Accessories

6. FELNADIYT = 6. DEFIANTLY
   In a manner rejecting authority

7. CIROOVEPTLVYA = 7. PROVOCATIVELY
   In an exciting or stimulating way

8. NICGNMI = 8. MINCING
   Walking with short steps

9. OORRRTEPIP = 9. PROPRIETOR
   Owner

10. ATDRNESEU = 10. SAUNTERED
    Strolled

11. NIORTTEC = 11. CONTRITE
    Sorry

12. DRSCNIOTNPE = 12. NONDESCRIPT
    Having no individual, distinguishing characteristics

13. NAOMAIRCP = 13. PANORAMIC
    With a wide view

14. EDMEGER = 14. EMERGED
    Came out

15. CMGNLYAIEN = 15. MENACINGLY
    Threateningly

The Grapes of Wrath Vocabulary Juggle Letters 4

1. CTEUNYULRLT = 1. _____
   Fiercely

2. RNSEKATNCUOA = 2. _____
   Ill-tempered; difficult to handle

3. IEUINCSSVVOAS = 3. _____
   Liveliness; animation

4. AAISDSLE = 4. _____
   Assaulted

5. ILYTLEH = 5. _____
   Gracefully

6. NILYUNIIQRG = 6. _____
   Questioningly

7. REDMEU = 7. _____
   Shy; modest; reserved

8. REFAL = 8. _____
   Wild; savage

9. SELRLTSUSE = 9. _____
   Dull

10. EWDEIZN =10. _____
    Withered; wrinkled

11. PIERAPONENHS =11. _____
    Anxiousness

12. TNFILYEAD =12. _____
    In a manner rejecting authority

13. LABTIIONOG =13. _____
    Duty; contract; promise

14. IETDF =14. _____
    Stinky; smelly

15. RPYTOCEHI =15. _____
    One who says he believes one way but in action shows he believes the opposite

The Grapes of Wrath Vocabulary Juggle Letters 4 Answer Key

1. CTEUNYULRLT = 1. TRUCULENTLY
   Fiercely

2. RNSEKATNCUOA = 2. CANTANKEROUS
   Ill-tempered; difficult to handle

3. IEUINCSSVVOAS = 3. VIVACIOUSNESS
   Liveliness; animation

4. AAISDSLE = 4. ASSAILED
   Assaulted

5. ILYTLEH = 5. LITHELY
   Gracefully

6. NILYUNIIQRG = 6. INQUIRINGLY
   Questioningly

7. REDMEU = 7. DEMURE
   Shy; modest; reserved

8. REFAL = 8. FERAL
   Wild; savage

9. SELRLTSUSE = 9. LUSTERLESS
   Dull

10. EWDEIZN = 10. WIZENED
    Withered; wrinkled

11. PIERAPONENHS = 11. APPREHENSION
    Anxiousness

12. TNFILYEAD = 12. DEFIANTLY
    In a manner rejecting authority

13. LABTIIONOG = 13. OBLIGATION
    Duty; contract; promise

14. IETDF = 14. FETID
    Stinky; smelly

15. RPYTOCEHI = 15. HYPOCRITE
    One who says he believes one way but in action shows he believes the opposite

ACCOUTERMENTS	Accessories
AGITATORS	People who stir up trouble
ALOOF	Reserved; distant
ANLAGE	Initial cell structure from which a part or organ develops; foundation
APPREHENSION	Anxiousness
ASSAILED	Assaulted

BESEECH	Make an earnest request
CANTANKEROUS	Ill-tempered; difficult to handle
CONCESSION	Compromise
CONQUEST	Accomplishment; having overcome something
CONSERVED	Saved; used sparingly
CONTRITE	Sorry

CULVERT	Drainage ditch
CYNICAL	Scornful of the motives, virtue or integrity of others
DECLIVITY	Slope; hill
DEFIANTLY	In a manner rejecting authority
DEMURE	Shy; modest; reserved
DENUNCIATION	Public condemnation

DISCONSOLATE	Dejected; gloomy
EMERGED	Came out
ENGAGINGLY	Charmingly; attractively
ENGULFED	Swallowed up; surrounded; enclosed
ENSNARED	Caught
EXHORTATION	Speech intended to advise, incite or encourage

FATUOUSLY	Smugly
FERAL	Wild; savage
FETID	Stinky; smelly
FORLORN	Sad because of being abandoned
FRET	Worry
HYPOCRITE	One who says he believes one way but in action shows he believes the opposite

IMPERIOUSLY	Authoritatively
IMPERTURBABLE	Can't be upset or annoyed
INQUIRINGLY	Questioningly
INSIGNIA	Emblem
IRRITABLY	In a manner showing annoyance
LECHEROUS	Tending towards excessive promiscuous behavior

LINGERED	Remained; tarried
LITHELY	Gracefully
LUSTERLESS	Dull
LUXURIOUSLY	As an indulgence; not necessarily out of necessity
MENACINGLY	Threateningly
MINCING	Walking with short steps

MODULATED	With a varying tone
NEBULOUS	Lacking definite form
NONDESCRIPT	Having no individual, distinguishing characteristics
OBLIGATION	Duty; contract; promise
OBSCURED	Hidden from view
OSTRACISM	Being shunned or ignored by the group

PALL	Gloomy atmosphere
PANORAMIC	With a wide view
PARADOXES	Seemingly contradictory aspects
PERPLEXITY	Confusion; puzzlement
PINNACLES	Tall, pointed formations
PRECINCT	District

PRECIOUS	Valuable
PRODIGAL	Extravagant
PROPRIETOR	Owner
PROVOCATIVELY	In an exciting or stimulating way
PUTRESCENCE	Rotten, decaying matter
RAVENOUS	Extremely hungry

REASSURED	Restored confidence
RECEDED	Withdrew
SAUNTERED	Strolled
SERENE	Calm, peaceful
SKULK	Lurk; lie in hiding
SULKILY	Gloomily; in a withdrawn manner

TAUT	Tight; tense
TIMBRE	Distinguishing quality of a sound
TRUCULENTLY	Fiercely
VAGUE	Not clearly expressive
VITALITY	Energy; liveliness
VIVACIOUSNESS	Liveliness; animation

WIZENED | Withered; wrinkled

The Grapes of Wrath Vocabulary

DEMURE	DENUNCIATION	PRODIGAL	ENGULFED	INQUIRINGLY
LUSTERLESS	PRECIOUS	VIVACIOUSNESS	LITHELY	CYNICAL
CONCESSION	FORLORN	FREE SPACE	TRUCULENTLY	FRET
RECEDED	PARADOXES	ALOOF	MENACINGLY	LECHEROUS
TAUT	NONDESCRIPT	FATUOUSLY	FETID	ACCOUTERMENTS

The Grapes of Wrath Vocabulary

CULVERT	DECLIVITY	VITALITY	PANORAMIC	SKULK
OSTRACISM	REASSURED	ENSNARED	VAGUE	DEFIANTLY
PINNACLES	PROVOCATIVELY	FREE SPACE	IMPERTURBABLE	PALL
RAVENOUS	MINCING	DISCONSOLATE	INSIGNIA	TIMBRE
IRRITABLY	LINGERED	ASSAILED	EMERGED	EXHORTATION

The Grapes of Wrath Vocabulary

CONQUEST	FRET	VAGUE	OSTRACISM	CANTANKEROUS
TIMBRE	ANLAGE	IRRITABLY	LECHEROUS	PERPLEXITY
APPREHENSION	LINGERED	FREE SPACE	HYPOCRITE	ENGAGINGLY
CONCESSION	SKULK	ENSNARED	RAVENOUS	PINNACLES
DECLIVITY	ASSAILED	CYNICAL	PUTRESCENCE	MENACINGLY

The Grapes of Wrath Vocabulary

IMPERIOUSLY	LUSTERLESS	INQUIRINGLY	FORLORN	SAUNTERED
WIZENED	EMERGED	REASSURED	FETID	IMPERTURBABLE
PALL	NONDESCRIPT	FREE SPACE	LUXURIOUSLY	PRODIGAL
MINCING	PRECIOUS	TRUCULENTLY	PRECINCT	DISCONSOLATE
DEMURE	OBSCURED	RECEDED	CONSERVED	ENGULFED

The Grapes of Wrath Vocabulary

ANLAGE	BESEECH	SERENE	OBLIGATION	SULKILY
CONCESSION	DEFIANTLY	DENUNCIATION	FRET	VITALITY
VIVACIOUSNESS	WIZENED	FREE SPACE	IMPERIOUSLY	PUTRESCENCE
PANORAMIC	ENSNARED	TIMBRE	ENGAGINGLY	IRRITABLY
TRUCULENTLY	ENGULFED	INQUIRINGLY	EMERGED	OSTRACISM

The Grapes of Wrath Vocabulary

REASSURED	NONDESCRIPT	PRECINCT	CULVERT	RAVENOUS
DEMURE	MINCING	PALL	HYPOCRITE	CYNICAL
MODULATED	PARADOXES	FREE SPACE	CONTRITE	LINGERED
CONSERVED	CANTANKEROUS	FETID	ASSAILED	APPREHENSION
DECLIVITY	LUXURIOUSLY	VAGUE	INSIGNIA	OBSCURED

The Grapes of Wrath Vocabulary

PINNACLES	ENGAGINGLY	MODULATED	ENSNARED	ANLAGE
IMPERTURBABLE	REASSURED	CULVERT	EMERGED	DENUNCIATION
CYNICAL	VITALITY	FREE SPACE	FETID	LUXURIOUSLY
LUSTERLESS	NEBULOUS	TRUCULENTLY	SERENE	INSIGNIA
AGITATORS	VIVACIOUSNESS	LECHEROUS	RAVENOUS	NONDESCRIPT

The Grapes of Wrath Vocabulary

PANORAMIC	PUTRESCENCE	FRET	DISCONSOLATE	MINCING
OSTRACISM	WIZENED	RECEDED	HYPOCRITE	FORLORN
INQUIRINGLY	TAUT	FREE SPACE	CONQUEST	CONCESSION
ALOOF	PALL	FATUOUSLY	CANTANKEROUS	LINGERED
PROVOCATIVELY	MENACINGLY	ACCOUTERMENTS	PARADOXES	CONTRITE

The Grapes of Wrath Vocabulary

PINNACLES	PARADOXES	OBSCURED	RAVENOUS	EMERGED
LECHEROUS	ACCOUTERMENTS	TRUCULENTLY	PALL	ENSNARED
PROPRIETOR	SKULK	FREE SPACE	FETID	WIZENED
ENGULFED	BESEECH	FERAL	FRET	INQUIRINGLY
PRECINCT	CONCESSION	TIMBRE	LINGERED	SERENE

The Grapes of Wrath Vocabulary

IMPERTURBABLE	CYNICAL	EXHORTATION	TAUT	MINCING
LITHELY	DEFIANTLY	OBLIGATION	PRECIOUS	INSIGNIA
DECLIVITY	DEMURE	FREE SPACE	IRRITABLY	SULKILY
OSTRACISM	NEBULOUS	MODULATED	VIVACIOUSNESS	NONDESCRIPT
FATUOUSLY	ENGAGINGLY	IMPERIOUSLY	PANORAMIC	LUSTERLESS

The Grapes of Wrath Vocabulary

FORLORN	ACCOUTERMENTS	IRRITABLY	LECHEROUS	FRET
PALL	CYNICAL	REASSURED	OBLIGATION	PROPRIETOR
PRECIOUS	PINNACLES	FREE SPACE	NONDESCRIPT	INQUIRINGLY
AGITATORS	HYPOCRITE	FATUOUSLY	RAVENOUS	VIVACIOUSNESS
PRECINCT	MINCING	CANTANKEROUS	CONSERVED	DENUNCIATION

The Grapes of Wrath Vocabulary

LINGERED	INSIGNIA	PERPLEXITY	CULVERT	DEFIANTLY
PRODIGAL	OSTRACISM	EXHORTATION	APPREHENSION	IMPERTURBABLE
ASSAILED	MENACINGLY	FREE SPACE	TAUT	WIZENED
SERENE	VITALITY	BESEECH	SKULK	ALOOF
EMERGED	DISCONSOLATE	PARADOXES	CONCESSION	IMPERIOUSLY

The Grapes of Wrath Vocabulary

SKULK	VIVACIOUSNESS	TAUT	DECLIVITY	WIZENED
INQUIRINGLY	SAUNTERED	PRECIOUS	CULVERT	CONCESSION
ENGULFED	DEMURE	FREE SPACE	ACCOUTERMENTS	OBLIGATION
CANTANKEROUS	ENSNARED	LITHELY	PROVOCATIVELY	CONQUEST
FERAL	ALOOF	NEBULOUS	ANLAGE	INSIGNIA

The Grapes of Wrath Vocabulary

MINCING	PRECINCT	OSTRACISM	IRRITABLY	LINGERED
PRODIGAL	AGITATORS	OBSCURED	BESEECH	VITALITY
FORLORN	CYNICAL	FREE SPACE	EXHORTATION	SERENE
PARADOXES	LUSTERLESS	PERPLEXITY	RECEDED	NONDESCRIPT
DEFIANTLY	ASSAILED	DENUNCIATION	SULKILY	REASSURED

The Grapes of Wrath Vocabulary

LUXURIOUSLY	BESEECH	ENGAGINGLY	FATUOUSLY	ENGULFED
IRRITABLY	OSTRACISM	DEFIANTLY	WIZENED	ACCOUTERMENTS
CONSERVED	LINGERED	FREE SPACE	VAGUE	MENACINGLY
PROPRIETOR	CONTRITE	VIVACIOUSNESS	CULVERT	DENUNCIATION
MODULATED	IMPERIOUSLY	SULKILY	FETID	LITHELY

The Grapes of Wrath Vocabulary

NONDESCRIPT	DISCONSOLATE	FRET	HYPOCRITE	TIMBRE
DECLIVITY	ANLAGE	FORLORN	LUSTERLESS	PANORAMIC
ENSNARED	RAVENOUS	FREE SPACE	CANTANKEROUS	INSIGNIA
EXHORTATION	RECEDED	ALOOF	INQUIRINGLY	PALL
APPREHENSION	PERPLEXITY	OBSCURED	PUTRESCENCE	DEMURE

The Grapes of Wrath Vocabulary

TRUCULENTLY	CONQUEST	FATUOUSLY	EXHORTATION	IRRITABLY
ALOOF	FETID	NEBULOUS	RECEDED	PINNACLES
ENSNARED	DEFIANTLY	FREE SPACE	MODULATED	SULKILY
TIMBRE	ENGAGINGLY	PERPLEXITY	IMPERTURBABLE	CULVERT
LITHELY	DEMURE	LINGERED	DISCONSOLATE	FRET

The Grapes of Wrath Vocabulary

PROPRIETOR	VIVACIOUSNESS	HYPOCRITE	WIZENED	CONTRITE
PRODIGAL	APPREHENSION	OBSCURED	EMERGED	FORLORN
TAUT	AGITATORS	FREE SPACE	ACCOUTERMENTS	DENUNCIATION
CONCESSION	OBLIGATION	DECLIVITY	ANLAGE	ASSAILED
REASSURED	OSTRACISM	ENGULFED	LECHEROUS	NONDESCRIPT

The Grapes of Wrath Vocabulary

LECHEROUS	FATUOUSLY	IMPERTURBABLE	DENUNCIATION	IMPERIOUSLY
OSTRACISM	HYPOCRITE	NEBULOUS	EXHORTATION	TAUT
DISCONSOLATE	MODULATED	FREE SPACE	DECLIVITY	ACCOUTERMENTS
PUTRESCENCE	CONTRITE	LITHELY	ANLAGE	INQUIRINGLY
RAVENOUS	ALOOF	CANTANKEROUS	PANORAMIC	SKULK

The Grapes of Wrath Vocabulary

WIZENED	LINGERED	PINNACLES	ENGAGINGLY	INSIGNIA
FETID	FORLORN	PALL	VIVACIOUSNESS	OBSCURED
IRRITABLY	SAUNTERED	FREE SPACE	DEMURE	VAGUE
PROVOCATIVELY	TRUCULENTLY	REASSURED	FERAL	VITALITY
SULKILY	PRODIGAL	NONDESCRIPT	CULVERT	APPREHENSION

The Grapes of Wrath Vocabulary

ENGAGINGLY	PARADOXES	PALL	TIMBRE	DEMURE
WIZENED	OSTRACISM	SERENE	CYNICAL	LUSTERLESS
FERAL	AGITATORS	FREE SPACE	VAGUE	RECEDED
FRET	IMPERTURBABLE	PANORAMIC	NONDESCRIPT	SULKILY
FORLORN	ANLAGE	CONSERVED	CONTRITE	DENUNCIATION

The Grapes of Wrath Vocabulary

CANTANKEROUS	CULVERT	CONQUEST	SKULK	IMPERIOUSLY
APPREHENSION	ENGULFED	INQUIRINGLY	EXHORTATION	LITHELY
NEBULOUS	FETID	FREE SPACE	CONCESSION	ACCOUTERMENTS
FATUOUSLY	PUTRESCENCE	MODULATED	TRUCULENTLY	IRRITABLY
OBSCURED	LUXURIOUSLY	PRECIOUS	PERPLEXITY	BESEECH

The Grapes of Wrath Vocabulary

DECLIVITY	APPREHENSION	IMPERIOUSLY	IMPERTURBABLE	RAVENOUS
TIMBRE	CYNICAL	NONDESCRIPT	TAUT	TRUCULENTLY
FERAL	LITHELY	FREE SPACE	PROVOCATIVELY	PERPLEXITY
MENACINGLY	ENGAGINGLY	WIZENED	PROPRIETOR	CONTRITE
LECHEROUS	INQUIRINGLY	FATUOUSLY	SKULK	VITALITY

The Grapes of Wrath Vocabulary

ALOOF	VIVACIOUSNESS	CONCESSION	CONQUEST	HYPOCRITE
ASSAILED	FRET	DEMURE	CONSERVED	PRECINCT
RECEDED	FORLORN	FREE SPACE	PARADOXES	ANLAGE
ACCOUTERMENTS	MINCING	IRRITABLY	OBSCURED	ENSNARED
INSIGNIA	OBLIGATION	SAUNTERED	CULVERT	PINNACLES

The Grapes of Wrath Vocabulary

CONTRITE	ACCOUTERMENTS	PALL	PRECIOUS	CONQUEST
SAUNTERED	PARADOXES	APPREHENSION	HYPOCRITE	OSTRACISM
INQUIRINGLY	MINCING	FREE SPACE	SKULK	NEBULOUS
SERENE	VIVACIOUSNESS	DEFIANTLY	MODULATED	MENACINGLY
OBSCURED	CULVERT	FRET	PUTRESCENCE	PROPRIETOR

The Grapes of Wrath Vocabulary

PRODIGAL	NONDESCRIPT	PROVOCATIVELY	RECEDED	FATUOUSLY
OBLIGATION	VITALITY	ENGAGINGLY	RAVENOUS	ANLAGE
FETID	PINNACLES	FREE SPACE	AGITATORS	SULKILY
VAGUE	ALOOF	PRECINCT	INSIGNIA	DENUNCIATION
ASSAILED	TRUCULENTLY	FORLORN	CANTANKEROUS	IMPERTURBABLE

The Grapes of Wrath Vocabulary

SULKILY	OBLIGATION	MODULATED	AGITATORS	LUXURIOUSLY
IMPERTURBABLE	SAUNTERED	CULVERT	DEFIANTLY	ENSNARED
ASSAILED	PERPLEXITY	FREE SPACE	MENACINGLY	NEBULOUS
CONQUEST	ANLAGE	PUTRESCENCE	REASSURED	PANORAMIC
TRUCULENTLY	INQUIRINGLY	RECEDED	ENGAGINGLY	PARADOXES

The Grapes of Wrath Vocabulary

FORLORN	VIVACIOUSNESS	SKULK	TIMBRE	IMPERIOUSLY
BESEECH	CONCESSION	VAGUE	MINCING	EMERGED
CONSERVED	PRECIOUS	FREE SPACE	FRET	CONTRITE
ACCOUTERMENTS	EXHORTATION	LINGERED	PRECINCT	PROPRIETOR
DENUNCIATION	RAVENOUS	DECLIVITY	OBSCURED	INSIGNIA

The Grapes of Wrath Vocabulary

ENGAGINGLY	ENSNARED	PRECIOUS	HYPOCRITE	CONCESSION
PRODIGAL	IRRITABLY	SULKILY	ENGULFED	DEFIANTLY
EXHORTATION	LINGERED	FREE SPACE	ALOOF	CONTRITE
CULVERT	MENACINGLY	OBLIGATION	NONDESCRIPT	LUXURIOUSLY
ASSAILED	CONQUEST	REASSURED	CYNICAL	PERPLEXITY

The Grapes of Wrath Vocabulary

RAVENOUS	DENUNCIATION	MINCING	FRET	DISCONSOLATE
MODULATED	SKULK	FORLORN	SAUNTERED	WIZENED
FATUOUSLY	LITHELY	FREE SPACE	DECLIVITY	PRECINCT
PALL	OSTRACISM	OBSCURED	EMERGED	FERAL
DEMURE	RECEDED	PINNACLES	SERENE	BESEECH

The Grapes of Wrath Vocabulary

TAUT	TRUCULENTLY	SERENE	SULKILY	CONTRITE
ASSAILED	BESEECH	OBSCURED	SAUNTERED	ANLAGE
PROVOCATIVELY	OSTRACISM	FREE SPACE	FATUOUSLY	RAVENOUS
VIVACIOUSNESS	NEBULOUS	PARADOXES	IRRITABLY	SKULK
WIZENED	DECLIVITY	FETID	LINGERED	INQUIRINGLY

The Grapes of Wrath Vocabulary

DEMURE	EXHORTATION	EMERGED	INSIGNIA	ENGULFED
LUXURIOUSLY	IMPERIOUSLY	CYNICAL	PERPLEXITY	LITHELY
CANTANKEROUS	CONSERVED	FREE SPACE	MINCING	REASSURED
FORLORN	MENACINGLY	NONDESCRIPT	VAGUE	OBLIGATION
LECHEROUS	PANORAMIC	DENUNCIATION	FERAL	CONCESSION